Songs
of Revolution

Curated by
Rebecca Rijsdijk

For the oppressed,
and the ones fighting oppression.

Stripped

All the babies have died
while you spent all that time
intellectualising genocide.

— Nina Nazir

Introduction

In the solemn halls of the International Court of Justice, a new chapter unfolds in the ongoing narrative of global discord. As the World Court, led by President Judge Joan Donoghue, makes a pivotal ruling on the conflict between Israel and Gaza, the echoes of history resonate through our present. This moment, bridging past and present, sets the stage for "Songs of Revolution"—an anthology born from the urgent cries of a world grappling with the legacies of colonialism, imperialism, and the unyielding quest for justice.

"Songs of Revolution" is not merely a collection of words; it is a journey into the heart of human emotion, charting a course through the scars of conflict and survival. In these pages, we confront the haunting legacies of empires, their enduring influence over contemporary crises, as vividly illustrated by the recent events in Gaza and Israel. The anthology delves into these narratives, offering a window into the resilience of the human spirit amidst the tides of history.

The story of the conflict, as reflected in the recent World Court ruling, is a testament to the complex interplay of power, justice, and human rights. The court's decision, while falling short of ordering a ceasefire, nonetheless represents a significant legal stance against acts of genocide, echoing the urgent need for humanitarian aid and the protection of civilians, as emphasised by Judge Donoghue. In alignment with this spirit, "Songs of Revolution" demands a permanent ceasefire now, calling for an end to the cycles of violence and the beginning of lasting peace.

This modern era, marked by the spectre of neo-colonialism, sees global powers continuing to wield influence, often under the guise of globalisation and aid. The anthology probes into these contemporary manifestations of imperialism, as seen in the World Court's call for accountability and the international community's reaction to the plight of Palestinians and the defensive stance of Israel.

Each poem and story in "Songs of Revolution" is a testament to the ongoing struggles born from historical injustices. They are intimate portraits of individuals and communities, not just fighting for survival, but for the right to voice their own, unbridled songs of revolution.

Amidst the backdrop of the World Court's recent ruling, the ongoing bombardment in Khan Younis, and the silent vigils for those lost, this anthology stands as a witness to the enduring pain and resilience birthed from the long shadows of history. Yet, within this tapestry of sorrow and struggle, a thread of hope persists—a belief in the power of solidarity and human connection to challenge and transcend deep-rooted injustices.

"Songs of Revolution" is more than an anthology; it's a catalyst for introspection and action. It urges us to understand the roots of current conflicts in a colonial and imperial past, to recognise our collective role in shaping a future informed by these lessons. As we immerse ourselves in these pages, we are called not just to read, but to empathise, question, and act— to be part of a journey towards a world where past empires no longer dictate our destiny and where a permanent ceasefire heralds the start of a new era of peace and unity.

Through this literary voyage, we seek to ignite a flame of change, a movement towards a world where songs of revolution become anthems of peace and unity, where the fragmented narratives of history find solace in a chorus of collective healing and hope.

Rebecca Rijsdijk,
Chief of Everything,
Sunday Mornings at the River

Smitten

by ALSHAAD KARA

Nightfall is not enough
To end the martyrdom
Caused by the fireplace
Lashed by the heart.

This thirst to be by your side
Is a never-ending melody
Darted with dire pain.

Such insolence is a
Continuous downpour
Which my unrequited love
Enjoys in this lonely twilight.

"In Time"

by MAUREEN TAÑADA

Shrills of terror climbing up the strands of time,
Tangling it more than ever.
Grief ever so repressed, moving in time and space,
In this living hell drenched in missiles whistling and the
bellowing of bombs.

The shingles on the children, regardless of age,
Lay on plastic covers under the overcast of stench and
looming flies.
Words in their mother tongue weigh on top of the eyes
that say it all,
Eyes that never sleep, now sealed shut, some eyes lifelessly
white with gaping mouths.
Was there anybody from the other side who could hear
me?
Beyond the barbed wires and the cries for Allah above?
I'm here under the crashing waves of rubble, flicking my
eyes.
From this, would my eyes be opened towards the future of
love, compassion, and peace?
Where I can co-exist as a person without gunpowder or
gas dancing in the air, my siblings giggling as they play
with neighbours from the next house, where I can hope
that dreams can and would still exist.
Ya Allah!
Hear us.

little bell to ding

by ROY DUFFIELD

late for the protest
I took a city bike – hadn't been paying attention
to the signs, ignored
each red light – it was only
when I saw the police
driving right for me, I realised (due to public
cuts) it had no brakes –
as I prepared
for head-on collision
(with only this little bell to ding)
I couldn't stop
this movement

Even if I'd wanted to

The Watermelon Struck City

by AHMAD MORID

In the city where watermelons burst like bombs,
And stain the sky red
Where streets drown in juices of crimson and seed,
Children's laughter is etched into the walls and
reverberates through the land
And life sprouts defiantly from war's deed
Here, buildings wear scars, yet stand proud and tall,
Against the sky's canvas, they paint a tale,
Of resilience, a city that won't fall,
In the face of despair, they refuse to pale.
The watermelon struck city, bold and bright
Holds stories of sorrow, yet sings of hope,
In each slice of life, in each day and night
Its people have the strength, with fate, to cope.
In this watermelon garden, every seed is a dream,
soon sprouting higher than the heavens
In the heart of destruction, life's new theme

the hand that rocks the cradle

by TETYANA DENFORD

the hand that rocks the cradle
rules the world.
isn't that the saying?
I whisper that when
I see a woman in front of me
in the grocery store checkout line
and I wonder if she thinks of death
as she holds a loaf of bread and milk
while soothing the baby beside her
does she realise her luck
that there are no bombs whistling in Aisle 3
there are no sounds of
gurney wheels
squeaking under the weight of grief
only the sound of relief
and laughter
when the baby suddenly wakes
and I wonder if she knows
that in some places there are no hopeful stories,
no world to rule, no fables,
just empty cradles
and a world rocking on its axis
hungry to see
a sun that still rises for
as if everyone was free.

Ashamed

by ANNE FEY

There is an ancient story
God disliked his creation of mankind
So he flooded the entire world
Only one family survived

If I lived in Noah's time
And this is what it was like
I would pray to God, please,

By all means, bring on those rains
Don't hold back. Drown the lot.
And reconsider that ark.

To the Zionists in the Room and All Their Cousins

by JUDE RAED

To the Zionists in the Room and All Their Cousins:
We Know Who You Are.
You Reek.
Like rotten maggots in a forgotten apple, on the kitchen
counter of long-past time.

What else can you do, staring at the gaping mouth of a
lion, but count its teeth?

Jagged, ragged, and impending. Inching closer.

To the Zionists in the Room and All Their Cousins, we
declare you UNACCEPTED.
Obscure the hidden translation of what it means to be
Palestinian, Sudanese, Black & Irish, Iraqi, Syrian, Libyan,
and Lebanese.

The COLOURnisers. Noetics cut shards into the body of
your lies and create cradles for you to sleep at night: in
your ears, you hear us scream:
To the Zionists in the Room and ALL Their Cousins, No.
You are not forgiven.
Your history, not forgotten.

This isn't a poem about Palestine, but if it were,
I would tell you how you murdered Christmas, how you lit
the sea on fire.
Santa Claus stands in the ruins of Ghazeh, looking for the
children.

Finds none.

The day you first saw your sister wrapped in white cloth
was not on her wedding day.
The day your mother met her fears was when you died –
hungry, small, cold, without a funeral, live on subscription
TV.
To the Zionists in the Room and All Their Other Cousins,
You ask to be forgiven, you lust-driven thieves, paper-
money demons of the world down-below, and you plead
the fifth; you plead innocence. All you do is plead, plead,
plead.

The side effects of too many side effects. The avalanche
of an avalanche,

Drugged-up American dream, white-picket-fenced banker.

You who spend every last penny at the dispensary of
Unanswered Confession,
Your god is paper money. Thin, anorexic, sick, Satan-
limbed. You pray to Capitalism, it spits at your feet.

Your altar arrives in a hearse of skeletons, the tears of the
guests bribed, the name of every child shoved down your
throat. You try to scream
But we quietly mourned louder,
20,000 martyrs
vs.
a billionaire, a casino heir, woefully ignorant and not ready
to meet God.

Meets Him anyway.

In response to being asked to write a poem to a generation
of poets, the
Martyr Son of a Martyred Son heaves heaven in and
answers none.
If I must die, you must live to tell my poems to the
orphanage, because there are no orphans left alive.

You must stand against the handles of time and declare
yourselves immortal. Nevertheless important, you must
disown defeat.
They will steal the skies from you, if they can they have
and they will, they will steal your sea, they will steal your
dirt and your graveyards, your temporal future, borderline
apocalyptic, annihilistic, perpetrator of the damned, gasps
in progressive symbology and paves a path towards being,
between being, towards un-being, and now—
You must see—
The sun—
Collapse.

Surrender yourself to the cosmos.
You're convinced a revolution is a revolution only because
it's temporary,
& then,
Had you believed the dark worn blindness as if it were
madness, stuck its elbows out the void and into the light
reborn, stumbles against itself and takes a swig of Reiki
punk rock straight from the bottle,
You must suppose the future bent and hid itself,
Suppose it has risen betrayal,
Suppose it had overridden fear.
You limp.
Sometimes you carry shame and a cane, sometimes you
disappear.
You who were once named quicktongue, quickdreamt,
halfsung;
You who were once named unexpected, uncemented,
taught-wrung,

Do you think this monologue was accidental?
What makes you an animal? What has you trapped?
This is not a poem about Palestine.
If it were,
I would have told you that our sky is not held up by Atlas
but by belief, that time forever transitions from a guardian

angel to Dragons of Eden to drinking spacetime
continuum, to
Quantum theory being the cosmos daydreaming of its
long dead stars.
Zionists in this room and all your cousins,
The kids will bring all the ruckus
Connects tangerines of Falasteen to the womb-tombs of
mothers & knots knotted time clean.

This is a poem that dives in from Warsan Shire, Ghassan,
and Al-Areer.
They tell us not to write poetry that is political.
They tell us the diasporic community started off with just
one cultured man.

To hell with your civilised world, then, man,
We hum to the stolen beat of every footstep of those
kicked out from their homeland.
Every bit of semanticism, beat the algorithm into
submission,
unkept.
Spits out
all the Malcolms.
This is vexing. Equates silence to non-violence,
Perplexed, DC white saviour complex, the Ku Klux Klan,
Jim Jones, Herzl and the like, so to the Zionists in the
room and all their cousins, we know who you are.

You REEK—

And our Resistance

is SO STARVING

it finally EATS.

Reign Down on Me

by TONKABELL

It's 5 am, water rains down my window,
It drips softly on the roof tiles.
I look outside to my concrete jungle,
And see new buildings for miles.
My bed is warm, my windows intact,
My coffee pot makes me a fresh brew.
I shower in hot water and dress,
And skip off to see my crew.
Dogs run round the park all day,
People smile amongst the grime.
In my cloudy Mancunian dream,
Nothing is running out of time.
The transport bustles on its way,
Taking people everywhere.
The homeless man sleeps wherever,
And no one seems to care.

It's 6 am, bullets rain down my window,
The tiles don't live here anymore.
My concrete jungle is now rubble,
New buildings razed to the floor.
My bed is bricks, my windows gone,
Hot coffee seems so far away.
Showers of tears are all around,
My crew are all dead in a day.
A dog licks his human's face,
His shattered smile full of grime.
This is my Ukrainian nightmare,
And we are running out of time.
Transport here are heavy tanks,
Taking bodies broken and bare.
Everybody is now homeless here,
When will somebody care?

Everyone's Shame

by TONKABELL

Any one broken
Any one caught
Any one left
Everyone fought
No one conquered
No one saw
No one won
In any war
Everyone payed
Everyone lost
Everyone trusted
But at what cost
Nobody rescued
Nobody came
Nobody listened
Everyone's shame

Where We Were Different

by AVA MAHTAB

Our childhood was strikingly different from theirs.
We were covered in dust when we came home from play.
When children of Palestine go out to play,
they don't come back.
Our mothers would hug us when we cried,
hushing us to sleep with a sweet lullaby.
When they weep, people ask - Is this a lie?
They burst into bloody tears,
and they question - is this a lie?
And they cry until they die.
Yet, the world still wonders - was that all a lie?

Our backpacks had broken crayons and pencils,
forgotten like silly pledges of peace.
Their backpacks had broken bones and body parts
of siblings the world would soon forget.
We scribbled our names on school walls and notebooks.
Their names are written on their arms and backs,
like labelling potato sacks.
It is a land of many little things -
olives, dates, days, dreams, shelters,
children, food, and water.
Even the sun sprinkles into little pieces
and falls at night.
And their tiny skulls bounce with the river's ebb and flow,
like little moons dipping into red skies.

We also had many little things -
eclairs, coins, dice, and dolls.
But our dreams are no longer nominal;
they have evolved with us
and now resemble facts.
We were born in white-washed hospitals,

wrapped in a warm towel.
They were born at the edge of swords,
shrouded at birth.
Our youth was not crushed under the rubble,
snared in bombshells,
and shrunk to bullets.
It was indeed strikingly different from theirs.
We were plain children
whose cries were not pleas;
we feared ghosts, not guns.
We didn't smile in pain,
and we had no courage;
no one told us we needed it.
They smile while they bleed and laugh while embracing
death.
No one tells them
they don't need it either.

In Quest of Peace

AVA MAHTAB

She recited a fable as her tired eyes wept
breathing were characters as people lay dead
to a child who earned his dreams as he slept
cradled on his mother's lap, life is better in his head
In it, there is shade, and in it, the sorrows fled

There is nothing to say; no one is left to hear
the sounds of destruction so loud
fear falls silent, and silent falls a tear
In quest of peace, they shot all the stars
While peace breathed last, bleeding through scars.

Please Put the Bombs Away

AVA MAHTAB

Please put the bombs away, let doves take flight,
In skies once torn by war's unyielding grasp,
Let peace descend, in gentle rays of light,
And in its warmth, let our united hearts clasp.

No more the sounds of sorrow, the cries of fear,
Let children's laughter be our guiding tune,
In every street, let hope wipe away the tear,
Under the watchful gaze of the benevolent moon.

Please put the bombs away, and with them, hate,
Let love's seed grow in lands once scarred and bare,
Together, let's open the future's gate,
With hearts entwined, a world rebuilt and fair.

In this plea, our dreams are interwoven,
Please put the bombs away, let peace be chosen.

Ivy Envelopes Auschwitz's Gate

by GIACOMO BOFFI

Ivy envelops Auschwitz's gate,
it enters the word "labour"
and exits the word "freedom".
Aleppo kept the old dictator
but hosts a new playground.
Kids jump with toys
and rusty gold guns.
In Kyiv, they have a drinking game
when the red sirens blast.
Teens can't stop laughing
as they rush into shelters.
Music from the yachts off Tel Aviv
mutes the noise of the iron dome.
BPMs are paired
with grey missiles' fall.
Where once there was Hiroshima
now there is still Hiroshima.
Medical students, bicycle lanes, war memorials.
Some people take selfies,
others leave prayers.

There are many Auschwitzes and many Hiroshimas.
History demands we know them
while the world,
the world keeps turning.
It lays a thin grass layer on dry-blooded ground.
Fields can be battlefields and then tulip fields
and then battlefields again.
The sky pours the rain evenly
on concentration camps and summer camps alike.

I don't know if there's a moral,

a message to be taken,
or a meaning to be found.
The night brings us dreams
and some mornings have no clouds.

And as we are made of
nuclear bombs and bubble gum,
I look in the mirror and I see
my son.

News Segment / Statistics of Genocide

by RAHUL SINGH

With the help of revolutionary science,
Israel has created a machine that
turns Palestinians into numbers under rubble.
Exactness is not terribly important;
we round it off to the nearest zero because
addition is less cumbersome
if you exclude the weight of each name.
There are too many numbers to keep track of anyway:
Men, women, children, patients, doctors,
paramedics, teachers, students, relief workers,
pastors, journalists, writers, and those in the West Bank.
The arrogance of each to demand their own list is baffling.
We'd lose track if we were to say number 4196
was the daughter of 2457 and 3356, sister of 434,
best friend to 1136, niece to 4195 and 2216,
granddaughter of 267...
you get the point.
It's easier this way, believe us.
When have we lied to you?
Anyway, in other news,
Taylor and Travis put relationship rumours to bed
with their first public smooch.

Resistance

by JODIE DUFFY

*Home Office has painted over Mickey Mouse murals at asylum
centre for lone children* – inews, July 2023

while they sleep or sit in their chambers
late into the night, let us gather
our arsenal, our weapons for this fight
bring your pens, your paintbrushes
pile up the paint cans and the palettes
sharpen your pencils, ready to draw

we will break into the dark, forgotten rooms
where they say the suffering does not
belong to us and can only be solved
by faceless process and blank walls
we will paint familiar friendly faces
on the concrete and the whitewash

sketch the outline of Mickey Mouse
fill it with colour, and Minnie too
think of all the Disney films our children love
how many times have we seen Frozen?
or Encanto, the Lion King, Toy Story?
all the characters we can draw from memory

bring plenty of pink to paint Peppa Pig
create a new mission for the Paw Patrol
while they use ever sharper words
we will blunt their claims to speak for us
soften the edges of the system with colour
paint wildflowers on the walls

plant dandelions in every crack
redecorate the ceilings to look like the sky

daub a vibrant welcome on every door
they cannot paint over them all
and for every picture that is removed
let us paint hundreds more

We Have Seen the Light

by JODIE DUFFY

We have been lured out without
a winter coat too many times
by the promising sunshine of early Spring
only for the harsh wind to scrape our bones.

we have been sold a programme
that creates a roaring fire on our screens
while we shiver in our extra jumpers
and leave the energy bill unopened.

We know the meaning behind
the neon signs and their promises
the shop fronts glowing red inside.

The beams that scan the Channel
are not always the eyes of lifeboats.

So, when you illuminate the buildings
across the capital, know this:

We no longer mistake light for warmth.

Untitled

by SONIA HADJ SAID

How can we begin to heal generational trauma,
The sole legacy recycled on this weary planet?
On my mother's side,
The wolf prowls our borders once again,
Granted a voice, a platform to unleash its growl.

On my father's side,
The oppressor stands right at our door,
Battering it down with the help of allies —
(Hold on, aren't they allies on my mother's side,
Yet treat my other heritage like unworthy scum?)

How do I explain
The involuntary shiver at the sound of Russian,
A reaction beyond my control?
How do I explain
The religion of my ancestors, profound and peaceful,
Marred only by a few rogues?

How are we, the children of such tangled roots,
Supposed to build a better world?

Blood Red Bone White Ice Blue

by JOSEPH NUTMAN

They all want to live forever
from feeble patriarch to upstart statesman

bloody digits fingering history
stained by-proxy by assent

sabre sharp fountain pens rattle
as they stab at declarations

forked tongues flick at microphones
stood reptile cold at the pedestal

after all – *offence is the best defence* –
that hollow point spins like a bullet

but whichever way you shoot it –
they're cool with carpet-bombing children

Becoming

by REBECCA M WINTER

When I was born I was not afraid.

I did not know my mouth was unholy
like my mother's before me,
and her mother's before her.

Around me are men who claim to speak for God.
Theirs is not a god I know.

There are days I still search for my place in the world
when I am already—impossibly and miraculously—
here.

When I write about loving and lusting
and waiting and burning
—all tongue and tooth and thigh—
it is a prayer.

My name in my lover's mouth is a prayer.

I arrived already with divine knowledge in me.
The art of beating.
The art of breathing.

I learned along the way the art of becoming
and how to brandish the names of the ones I love
like a crucifix in the darkest nights—
over and over—
the most sacred of hymns.

A heart made of stone trembles, still.

I do not belong to any god.
If you ask me what I believe in I will show you
a blossoming tree in the springtime.

Come—
I will show you a world where the fruit is not forbidden;
the knowledge, never unholy.

Who is tolling the bell? Listen—

somewhere in the deep water
between your prayer of *I don't want to die*
and the ocean spitting you back out
is the world answering, *It is not your time.*

It is not your time.

It is no sin to exist,
to let love grow over you slowly, like moss.
It is no sin to change, to start again.
Ask me to prove it and I'll show you the moon.

Cosmos

by REBECCA M WINTER

Lower your voice when you speak to me.

Cut out the bastard tongue that suggests
I am not

holy—
that my body, my being, is not

divine. Indeed, show me—
what exists that is more sacred?

I am of that which is formed in the stars.

I have the cosmos in me—
I am all of it.

Your shame will not shake me.

Look upon me and know divinity.
Look upon me and know love.

Holy Ground

by REBECCA M WINTER

They say blasphemy
is taking the Lord's name in vain,
but perhaps blasphemy
is kicking over an anthill, or
throwing your cigarette butts
onto holy ground—
both.

They say holy ground is a place
men have deemed to be
thus, but
perhaps what is truly sacred
is not the cathedral,
is not the temple,
erected by men,
but the spider's web,
the burrows,
the nests,
the tall grass and the trees,
the pond, filled with tadpoles.

The word of God does not come from
the mouths of men in pulpits, but
in the songs of the birds and
the whales,
the hiss of snakes
and hunchbacked cats.

Holy is the desert,
the mountain,
and the sea—
the forests—

the saplings in medians, clinging to life,
the flowering weeds thriving through
cracks in the pavement.
Holy is everywhere all at once, and

Righteousness is not only kneeling
in prayer,
righteousness is kneeling
to pick up the cigarette butts,
and braking for small things that skitter across roads.

We are not holier than the field mouse.

Let Dancing Shoes Fall Down The Sky

by MARCELLA CAVALLO

Everybody could leave
the underground shelters, grab each other
by the hand. They go in circles, shaking off
the horror and smiles return on tired faces.

In a dancer's soul there is never
silence, just in scared eyes, that saw too much.
The girl keeps her posture even while she says goodbye
to her aunt and cousin for an unknown time.

Carry, carry some of her backpack weight.
Play, play all the music in this world that will
help her forget.

Back home in Ukraine, her shiny dancing shoes
will wait for her return.[1]

---

[1] *This piece is dedicated to Arina, a 9-year-old girl I got to know in the refugee shelter in my hometown.*

Piano Chords Born In The Attic

by MARCELLA CAVALLO

The gentle touch of piano keys, a sound
that proves years of practice.
Melancholy covers me in a blanket, and soft
warmth unfolds in my stomach
as I listen to the music
of our new Ukrainian neighbours
crawling through the open window.

A wrong note, clumsy,
unexpected. The music stops.
I can hear the heavy hesitation.
Maybe it is a remembrance
of war horror in her mind's eye,
the one that you can never close.
Or a knot of homesickness that gets
tighter with each familiar note lingering
in the air. What if it is a song her parents loved
to hear in the living room, when they decided to open
the dusty flap of the piano after Sunday lunch,
when all that matters
was sitting around the wooden table, with peaceful
smiles on their lips.

The silence is drowned by birds chirping.
One second,
two seconds,
three seconds.
And then there it is, the courage
to continue, to start over again.

What I admire the most.

After Donne

by RYAN SCHULTE

I wonder if spiritually those descended from women and
poor women and women of colour and gay women and
men of colour and white ones too—who died of AIDS—
would, if offered a settler state and nukes, make a hundred
years of holocaust just because they could. then reagan,
like death, could be proud.

And Just For A Moment, The Leaflets Looked Like Doves Swooping Over Gaza

by FI DIGNAN

The white murmuration flutters with feathers of ash
The rush of black streaked sheets urging migration
Word birds fell like the hush before
utterance. Utter. Devastation heralding the dash
of the silent rush before the bomb push

The deepest blue shushes of sky
gush down the utter of bird words, falling
amongst the once green of olive and plum trees
The white murmuration flutters with feathers of ash

A harvest gathering in trees like fleece
How our eyes rest on those dumb bone birds
Thinking of bushes of shushing doves, a harvest of love
Before, before swishing down before
the silent rush before the bomb push

Slush at our feet like sleet, these sheets
leak the words of dumb bone birds of tomb
and gash. A harvest of history murmurs amongst
the white murmuration flutters with feathers of ash

The silent rush before the bomb push
streaked black the hush of ash-filled air
the dumb bone birds burnt to ash as just

for a moment we plead

for the harvest of history, for the bird words to land

in bushes of peace and the gush of fiery arcs
across the screen of black to be the stuttering flash
of shooting stars. We made a wish
before the bomb push

But the still white smoke flutters
with feathers of ash

Nest of Angels

by JULIAN BOND

Butterflies drift over the tall flowering grasses,
Alongside the paths that crisscross the ancient rocky
hillside.
Feet crush thyme and lemon balm,
Walking through the orchards
Of mangos, pomegranates, figs, walnuts, peaches, oranges,
lemons, and olives,
And the birdsong everywhere
Delightful, Paradise.

*

All is dark, the moon so grand tonight, an impassive
witness,
Waiting, forever waiting!
Watching,
A people walk without direction,
Living without aim except to remain, except to remain
living.

And when we walk, we bump into walls!
A security wall,
A wall for peace,
War and peace, peace is war,
War is peace, wall is peace!

My persecutors call me a witch!
Well, why not a witch, ready to fly over this awesome wall,
I'll make it puny, insignificant!
A caressing moon shining down on Occupied Hebron,
Ancient Palestine.
Palestine, how good it feels to say the name.
So let's fly high above this wall.

Leave behind these colonisers, settlers, their vicious ways,
And the Israeli army soldiers.
To Bethlehem, Jericho, Nablus, Jerusalem, Galilee, Haifa,
and Jaffa,
Let's not quibble that the Israelis call it Tel Aviv,
A beautiful land, spiked and tied down.

Moon bathing in sweet kisses!
Come!
Come with me!
High above the land,
Come, let's find out what cake they bake,
What facts on the ground they create,
What the world fails to see or feigns not to see.

But be careful,
There must be many bullets flying around here.

Follow the moon
Up, up, up, high above the wall,
Still dark,
Ghosts everywhere!
Even the ghosts are under curfew here!
The skies above Hebron are full of them!
Bullets and ghosts.

City of ghosts and ghouls, the streets empty, night is quiet
now,
Cats, dogs, and rats are the lead actors in our little play!
The streets slumber after the hard work of day,
Channelling gunfire and grief!
But now listen, listen to the mournful slumber,
Can you hear?
Listen –
Six million souls whisper from lidless graves,
Unwilling recruits to legitimise barbarity.
Soon it will be light,
We'll travel our land,

Taken by Jewish colonisers,
Gathering our harvest,
Leaving for us only the path to the graveyard.

Come see the light of nations at work,
Come see this land, its soil covered in blood,
Come, let's hop over this little fence, this apparition,
To meet our neighbours.
'Good fences make for good neighbours,' they tell us,
Building a wall so high,
Well, we are beyond it now,
Halfway to the moon!
Hebron, bony-framed, small below,
An apartheid city in an apartheid land.

Hear, the rooster crowing!
You don't hear it?! Listen more closely!
There, now you hear it! I bet you didn't know that
roosters see angels!
Well, it's true, when they are crowing it's because they've
spotted an angel!
And I'll tell you another thing,
Donkeys spot devils!
In fact, every time they are braying it's because they've
spotted one!
You don't believe me.
You Westerners, you know your problem is you think;
thinking literally is rational!

Look, here comes an angel!
Now will you believe me?!
Hello!
Hi!
What's your name?
Ayya!
Hello, Ayya!

Look, Ayya, the sun's coming up,

Feel its first beautiful rays,
Hear the donkeys down below, braying as the tanks pass
by!
They must be devils!
'Oh, you don't believe that old wives' tale, do you?'
All that stuff about angels!
'They're just braying because they're scared, that's all!'
'It's true, I tell you!'
'It is not!'

Donkeys, taxis for the wretched of the earth,
Bent-backed men and withered women climbing slowly
over fences and walls,
Avoiding snipers,
Creeping from backyard to backyard,
Carrying baskets and boxes,
Burglars in their own homes,
Criminals in their own land.

Hebron lies like an abused daughter,
Qalqilia, Tulkarem, city prisons,
Concentration camps for the New World Order,
A Shoah visited upon us by the Israelis!
And there is Gaza,
Oh, weep for Gaza!

"That's where I'm from!
Or should I say where I was from!
You want me to tell you my story?

Tell me, Ayya!

"Well, I was eight years old! I died nine months ago now,
the very day before the next school year was starting, how
about that for bad luck!
Safa, that's my eldest sister, she's sixteen and so beautiful,
my best friend, well she gave me some money to get

goodies from the shop! She always spoiled me. I knew it too and loved her all the more for it!

Well, I was on my bike and I was coming back from the shop, I had some crisps, popcorn, biscuits, for a feast!
Anyway, there'd been a tank firing from the settlement nearby but I didn't think much of it,
I was thinking of all the goodies I had in my hand and was riding carefully so as not to fall off the bike and drop them when bang, the tank shot me! What a surprise, dead immediately!"

"Well, I woke up later, up here, flying around above myself, both here and there; it's the maddest feeling.
I could see myself, still holding the sweets, you know I never got to eat them.
Anyway, you don't have much of an appetite up here!"
"And there I was, covered in blood, in hospital, horrible, and everyone around me sobbing,
My poor mother, Rowan, my Uncle Fat'hi, and beautiful Safa, screaming and screaming.
I didn't care for myself; I just wanted to comfort them, for them to be all right!
Funny, you know, in hospital, 'cause I'd wanted to be a doctor, I worked really hard at school to get good grades so I could be one when I grew up and help people, and now I was there and I couldn't!
Well, at least I died quickly! No suffering. Not everyone's so lucky."

"There are loads of kids up here!
You get to play tick a lot up here and hide and seek is loads of fun; there's so much space!
We travel all over, wherever we like; I never travelled when I was living.
I never realised there was so much to see!"

"The worst thing is how sad my mum and Uncle Fat'hi and Safa are. That's what makes me cry!

I visit them every evening when they have gone to bed.
They don't know I'm there, but sometimes they feel a presence,
But then they don't believe themselves!
I give my Mum a kiss; she shivers; she doesn't realise it's me!
Then I go and see my Uncle and play with his curly hair,
And then I go and see Safa, and I curl up with her quietly on the bed, so as not to disturb her while she sleeps. She sobs out my name,
I wish I could comfort her and tell her I'm alright. She's so beautiful, she always helped me with my homework, just so I could get the best marks in class!
And she'd always read me a bedtime story even though she was tired herself,
And when there was shooting, I'd run into her room and she would cover me up in her bed and tell me that I was safe, and then I'd go to sleep.
I wish I could tell her not to feel guilty that I'm dead."

"Well, that's enough of my story,
Come on then!
Or do you just want to keep talking forever?!"

The Palestinian sun is hot now,
What a beautiful smell! Breathe it in!
Oranges!
There's a farmer below, shouting up to us.

"They're good oranges!
Better than all the other oranges in the whole wide world!
And tastier!
You know why?"
Why?
"Because I planted them,
These trees, I harvested them,
I make the tree happy,
I am happy and the tree is happy,

We dance together, the trees and I!"
"And when I smell them,
They remind me of my land, of the breeze,
And I am thankful to God!"
His name is Auda!

Good-bye, Auda, take care!
Do not tell him of the crushed oranges to come,
Do not foretell of the uprooted trees, stolen, reflected in
his glistening eyes,
He stands surrounded by fences and wires,
As strangers pick the fruit of his lands,
Ssssh, sshh, no mention of guns, watchful, waiting, eager
guns.
In the 'War of the Oranges'.

You know, before my mother became shapeless,
Just the very mention of oranges would bring a smile to
her face,
Even exiled from her land, as she was.
Exiled from her orange trees!

*

See the shimmer!
Butterflies drift over the tall flowering grasses,
Alongside the paths that crisscross this ancient rocky
hillside!
Your feet crush thyme and lemon balm as you walk
through orchards,
Of mango, pomegranates, figs, and walnuts, peaches,
lemons, olives, and oranges.
And the birdsong everywhere,
Delightful, paradise,

Until the drone of bulldozers breaks through,
And we know we have reached the settlement!

This dog on a leash!
Whose bite is far worse than its bark.
A watchdog to guard over the Arabs!
The promised Holy Land, Ancient Israel,
An alibi for murder.
Wall and tower on hilltop, looming, threatening,
provoking, picking a fight.

A land without people, only cockroaches and snakes.
A land without people, that's what you saw when you
invaded our land.
Your glasses must have been very thick to miss a million
people!
Or maybe you only saw cockroaches and snakes.
Easy to kill a snake, crush a cockroach,
After all, their blood doesn't count as much as yours!

Are you tillers or conquerors?
Oh Israel, this oasis, making the desert bloom!
Didn't we make it bloom for 2000 years? Have you lost
your memory as well as your sight?
Oh Israel, we are not tourists in this land,
We are not tourists!

To Jenin!
And another 'Ground Zero'!
Not an American Ground Zero, this one Palestinian, so it
doesn't count.
See the refugee camp, every blood-stained stone amongst
the bulldozed rubble a witness to another massacre of the
Palestinian people, by the brute Sharon.

A 'Nest of Cockroaches', so he called it!
Look, look, at the old women cockroaches,
And there the old men cockroaches,
And the baby cockroaches, holding pencils and school
satchels in their hands,
Such clever cockroaches, studying at school!

The soldiers kill one and we give birth to another!
We give birth to cockroaches, defying nature!
Are you afraid of us cockroaches, crawling over you in
your hallucinations,
Your nightmares, pushing you into the sea?
Beware the nightmare scenario,
Peace!
Peace with the cockroaches?
There must be war,
And more war and war again,
Exterminate the Palestinian cockroaches.
One million Arab cockroaches are not worth one single
clean, nicely filed, exonerated Jewish fingernail,
So spoke one of your Rabbis.
So we are a 'Nest of Cockroaches', are we?
Well, all I see is a 'Nest of Angels', some living, some
dead,
All angels.
And such wise angels nowadays,
Wise Angels remember what happens to cockroaches
when you terrorise them and drive them off the land,
1948,
You drove ¾ of a million cockroaches away, give or take a
few,
And what's a few cockroaches to you, tell me?
Carrying only what they could carry, deeds to their homes
And their blessed front door keys safely round their necks,
Soon to return, so they thought, but they never did.

They never existed, these homes, did they?
Mythical homes, bulldozed away,
Village after village, reduced to rubble, covered over with
mounds of earth.
Covered over and covered up,
Swept away under your magnificent carpet,
Forgotten now, never existed, mythical, make-believe,
ssssssssh!
What homes?

There were no homes,
Lies, all lies!
Sweet dreams now in your new-found Paradise,
No Paradise lost, just one found.

So forgive us this time if we don't fly the nest,
Forgive us if this time we stay put.
And the only thing that the angels have to say this time is,
"We will stay here"!

*

Now let's fly over the wall,
To visit Fortress Israel,
Come quickly, come quickly, from New York and Russia,
Come quickly, before it is too late, for the sun is setting.
Land of the Fathers,
A convenient covenant,
Promised to the Hebrews by a Hebrew God,
Or was it the British Empire and the American Congress,
To the 'Chosen People'!
So who are we? The Unchosen People.

One people, One army, A third Kingdom.
Happy 56th Birthday!
Will you last a thousand years,
Or maybe only another twelve?
Oh, Israel, gangster amongst gangsters,
Why do you pretend to be a good cop?
Good cop, bad cop!
You are in the wrong film; there are only bad cops here.
Messenger for the Godfathers,
Corrupt Mercury, flying in from Washington on F-16s.
An assassin ready for another mafia hit!
Another liquidation, extermination, termination,
Assassinating our history, if only you could.

The master's watchdog, sniffing out trouble whilst they
pillage for oil,
In poor grieving Iraq, raped and humiliated.

The master's watchdog,
He feeds you and you bite.
One change of owner but you never let that bother you,
The Americans took you into their loving arms when the
British could no longer feed you.

This 'Promised Land',
Oranges and grapes replaced by rockets and guns,
This 'Rock of Israel'.
This pirate outpost of milk and honey,
Swept clean,
Cleansed, dirt and cockroaches all out of sight,
Rounded up in enclosure pens,
And six million testimonies falsified
In your immoral justifications.

*

We are blinded!
We are blinded,
The golden sun bouncing off the Dome of the Rock.
Eternal, indivisible, Jerusalem,
Divided and twisted tower,
Leaning corrupt tower,
"Someone's coming!"
Where? I don't see.
"You'll see!"

The sun has set on Jerusalem.
A fresh moon in the sky,
And once again, all the stars are kissing,
Let's fly higher,
Back to the moon,
Colder and colder,
Darker and darker,
Blue night begins.
Hello! Who are you?
Are you an angel?

"Excuse me, my lady!
I've been called some things in my time but never an
angel!
My name is Shlomo,
It means 'peace' and 'wisdom' in Hebrew!
Though I assure you, I am not wise,
And as for peace,
Well, I ask you…

"I imagine you wish to know what an old Jewish ghost like
me is doing,
Flying around over the land of Palestine, no?"

Well, you know, I went up the chimney, as they say, in
Auschwitz,
You've heard of there no doubt, in 1944.
Before there, I was in the Warsaw Ghetto, they had a wall
you know,
Still, you know all about walls I see!
Anyway, get to the point, get to the point!
So how did I end up over here?

Well, you know everyone seemed to be coming this way.
Britain and America had closed their borders,
Who wants the poor and the desperate anyway?!
Ghosts are no more imaginative than the living,
They see what choices they have and act accordingly.
You might say I was swept up by the events of the time.
Even a ghost needs a bit of living space!
Perhaps one thing Hitler and I agree upon!

You talk of angels and see them everywhere,
Would you like to hear a story about an angel I once saw,
a long time ago?
It's not a particularly nice story.

Very well,
What do you see over there?

It's for hanging people! A gallows.
One day in Auschwitz after a particular act of
disobedience,
As a punishment, the head of the Gestapo ordered for a
boy, picked out at random, to be hanged there.
Even the SS were worried about hanging this boy in front
of thousands of us,
Inmates.

The boy they chose, he had the face of an angel.
A sad-eyed angel, pale and silent,
Very calm so it seemed to us even when they put the
noose around his neck.
Well, it took this angel a whole half an hour to die,
hanging there.
Someone behind me shouted out 'Where is God, where is
He?'
We prisoners were forced to look at his face as he swung
there.
After he had died, the same man shouted out again 'I ask
you, where is God now?'
So, I turned around and said to the man, 'Where is God?
Why, there He is, hanging on the gallows, see.'
You know there is no God!
I should know, I've been dead for, oh, let me think now,
almost 60 years.
He's not here!
And there's no one else up here that can help you!

We claimed to be a light unto nations!
Look what they commit in our name, those rats!
Yes, there are Jewish rats amongst us!
Sharon, Netanyahu, Barak, Peres,
A military junta for rats!
A curse upon them.
A disgrace to the Jewish people.

Lebensraum,

Living space,
That's what the Nazis called it,
'Übermenschen' and 'Untermenschen'.
Supermen and subhumans.
These rats have made a 'Chosen People Über Alles'.
I was called a 'dirty Jew', you know, many times,
In the Warsaw Ghetto,
They called that a 'closed military zone', does that ring any bells?
Now when I listen below, I hear 'dirty Arabs' and 'two-legged beasts'!
I hear too many things that remind me of my childhood.
Shame on them!
A tortured people, traumatised and terrorised, cross the Mediterranean,
To do the same to others!
Olive tree destroyers, orange annihilators, water destroyers, killers of meadows.
Hiding yourself with barbed wire fences and walls,
Fleeing from the ghetto to return to the ghetto.
And when we were dying in the concentration camps, did America do anything for us then? No!
Britain perhaps? No!
They could have bombed it, put us out of our misery.
We were expendable, like so many exhaust fumes.
European banks traded on us,
The Zionists tried to waltz with the Nazis, did you know that?
I found that out later.
Did the Statue of Liberty welcome the tired and poor huddled mass of Jewish refugees to its shore?
Did we not yearn to breathe freely enough?
And did Big Ben chime democratically its concern?
No, no, no!
"We don't want them here!
Put them amongst the Arabs, let them serve us.
Insurance for us as we cast our eyes on the oil fields those damn Arabs have got."

Anyway, what do I know?
I'm just a sickly old Jewish ghost!
Soon it will be dawn.
Time to say 'Goodbye'!

Goodbye, Shlomo!

Come, let's get back to our prison before it's light,
Model prisoners make thrifty vampires,
Bats swooping over the land, glistening in the dark.
Israel, do you sleep soundly whilst Palestinians toss and
turn forever, stuck in a nightmare?
Indulged now, returned from your leisure palaces, discos,
theatres, restaurants,
Soundly sleeping, comforted by the ticking clock.
Tick-Tock, Tick-Tock, Tick-Tock, Tick-Tock,
The ticking clock.

Well, don't be surprised when Palestinian babies come to
blow it all up,
Tortured and humiliated lives traded in.
Don't be shocked when the starving come to take away
your appetite.
Everyone fights with their own abilities,
David takes on Goliath, once again,
So who now Goliath,
Who now David?
Not you with your Apache Helicopters, your Tomahawk
missiles!
Maybe our stone-throwing boys will beat down the
boasting Goliath,
Bring him crashing down to the floor!

Outrageous theatre, this dying, blood-strewn, body parts
in nightclubs,
But no show for our people, daily dead,
Our names not found on billboards,

No reviewer for us, our deaths, a non-event, not
happening.
Our houses crushed by the bulldozers, unreported,

Don't be confused when the whole thing comes crashing
down like some cheap Jerusalem wedding hall,
Ill-conceived, of poor foundation,
With only the lunatic Sharon and his robber-barons elect
dancing on the roofs as the pillars collapse.

Sleep blissfully Israel, but wake up soon!
Let us live in our land and there'll be no more bombs.
Our little babies are empty glasses; they can love or hate.
But children do not stay children long,
Occupation soon kills their smiles,
They cry for a while till the anger comes,
And then they are ready to visit you,
Little Angels of Death.
Will you daub your doors with our blood for this
Passover?
Our blood is our signpost calling us!

Or why not a Final Solution, then?
How to get rid of this cancerous growth off your paled
European skin?
Beware chemotherapy kills cancer and patient alike!

Oh Israel, prodigal son,
A stranger, 2000 years gone, now returning to boot in the
door,
Overturn our tables and throw us into the street,
Oh, Israel, 'Beacon of Nations',
Europe has taught you such bad manners!
Let's return to Hebron,
Back to where we started our journey.
See, the tank watching over us!
Soldiers, upon the roof, wait patiently their starring role.

Hebron, city of Arabs strangled to death by this tawdry
colony of 500 Jewish zealots,
Can you imagine, the arithmetic does not make sense.
Five hundred zealots strangling a whole city, like some
parasitic plant.

They look peaceful now, sleeping softly by their wives'
sides,
But their souls are contorted with dreams of killing,
Sweet dreams of pulling us out by the roots from their
beautiful paradise,
Harmful grass to be weeded out, annihilated.
To be beaten like donkeys,
Till we learn never to raise our heads,
Beat us like a dog until we leave them in peace!

Well, why should we leave, this is our land.
You leave.
So you build your wall,
You know they dance Tai Chi now on the Great Wall of
China,
And sell picture postcards of the Berlin Wall?
Do you think your wall will last longer?

Pushed up against the wall, with nowhere left to go.
Would you like us to go to an Indian reservation?
Maybe with the Aborigines,
To a black township perhaps,
Or would you prefer us as a museum piece?
In the Holocaust Museum,
Would that not be fitting?
But your dreams remain haunted,
'Oh God, please don't let them in, save us from them!'
Do you think we'll trade in our lives to play the willing
victim?
Is that what you want?
The right to abuse us without complaint?
The abused turned abuser.

What?
Do I see the abuser getting angry when a mirror is thrust
in front of his face,
Forcing him to watch his perverted actions!
The abuser has the cheek to get angry with his victim
when the child cries out for help,
Cries out in pain,
He wants to shut her up,
So that no one in the family knows what he's up to,
Carrying on abusing them all the more.
Shame on such perverted and wicked men.

That's enough now, you do go on!
You know I've a friend up here, Ahmed, he got shot as
well,
Well, he was telling us that when Israel's soldiers arrive for
service,
The Major takes out their hearts and puts a grenade in its
place!
And that's why they can kill children without feeling
anything,
And then when they go home to see their families, they
find their hearts waiting on a shelf for them,
And that's why they can kiss their children and be so nice
to them!

I've never really seen a soldier's face, not closely, what are
they like?
Faces, just like us! Some dark, some pale!
I wonder what the soldier who killed me looks like?!
I'd like to meet him and ask him why he wanted to kill me!
I'm only a child, how could I hurt him?

Anyway, I really must be going!
I want to see Safa before she wakes,
And give her a kiss!
Goodbye!

Goodbye, Ayya!
Quietly now, back to my house.
I don't want to disturb my persecutors, squatting on the roof,
On the lookout, but not for a witch!
Lost in their hate of others,

The moon looks on unblinkingly,
The world watches on, unblinking,
Moon people of America!
Moon people of Britain!
European Moon People.

Is it the moon that sends arms and tanks and helicopters to the Israelis?
Does the moon pay for the bombs that kill our children,
Does the moon shoot down our children in cold blood,
Jail and torture us?
Has the moon manufactured this drip-dropped genocide?
Is it 'moon people' that occupy our land?
Must we put the moon on trial
For crimes against humanity?
Since no one else is responsible, it must be the moon!

So, will you stand by whilst they continue to 'cleanse' us of what remains of our land?
Each day, busy bulldozers take away a little bit more.
Each day a new advance of the wall,
Cutting us off, sawing us up.
Just 'facts on the ground'.
No need to negotiate when you possess the 'facts on the ground'.
Just keep everything stoked up,
Just keep building the prison.

Is it only the moon which stands by as the tanks roll over our crushed bodies,

Breaking our limbs, blasting holes through the hearts of
our children?
Today, and day after day, is it only the moon that gazes
on, tight-lipped, vowed to silence?
Would the moon speak out tomorrow?

Softly lit in the moonlight,
The very same moon that shines upon you
Shines down upon us and finds us here!

How important it is to live and love!
How lovely is the moon!
How long it has been since I have loved!
Or been loved!
Sometimes I feel alone on this earth, like there is no one
there for me!
And you?
Would you be there for me?

The moon is setting,
Day is coming, wrapped now in the mists of dawn,
Another virgin day on our beautiful earth!
I shall stay here,
In Palestine,
Land of my birth.

The day has come,
And the moon takes its leave,
Now obscured in the mist.
And I, too, will leave you now,

*

Butterflies drift over the tall flowering grasses,
Alongside the paths that crisscross this ancient rocky
hillside.
Our feet crush thyme and lemon balm as we walk through
the orchards,

Of mangos, pomegranates, figs, walnuts, peaches, oranges,
lemons, and olives,
Listening to the birdsong everywhere,
Delightful, Paradise.

What Can I Do?

by CINDY J. STEWARD

They vanished for a day, maybe two,
and introspectives consumed the day,
the evening, the night, the morning.
Leaves of an early, maybe late, autumn
tainted the early rising and late sinking
sun, and I wondered why.

Questions circled my love, and affection
broke my heart in tiny little pieces, until
nothing was left for repetition, and they
returned.

"Sorry, sorry, sorry,"
"my uncle passed,"
"airstrike."

How we rose above ourselves
with a few words and phrases
that everyone has heard
and mean less than the
fall mud under my shoes.

Fresh air felt strangling,
suddenly, and
I could only utter
condolences.

Against All Odds and Soaring Waves

by FIDAN NAZIM

Every story I open has a trigger warning.
"We live in the triggering times," my colleague says.
Morning coffee burns my tongue,
as I stare at a photo of a tiny fist sticking out of the rubble.
My hand curls in a fist, too.

When my children enter the room, I hide my phone.
They can't see what I see.
Those children's horror is too much
for my kids to perceive.
My sandwich scratches my throat like glass when I swallow it.

"It's complicated," a friend says when we speak of Palestine,
"There are two sides to every story."
Her face twists in dismay when she sees the photo I show her.
Her body disagrees with her sentiment.
I should have given her a trigger warning.

I learn new things every day.
In Gaza death certificates are issued before birth ones.
Most children in the hospitals have a title scribbled on their skin –
WCNSF. Wounded Child with No Surviving Family.
Now how can I unlearn it?

When I look up, October sky is milky white and silent,
the way it should be.
I wish every child could trust the sky.
A little stone in my shoe digs into my foot,
I put more weight on it.

When I hug my daughter goodnight,
Her hands are warm, and her eyes are calm.
But then I see her scream under the rubble in a flash of
fear-induced madness,
and my chest turns to stone.

I write letters to Palestinian children on my lunch breaks.
They always start with 'My sweetheart', 'my darling', 'my
angel'.
They always end with 'I'm so sorry.'
When my partner asks me how work was,
I never remember.

Dr Ghassan of Gaza says he found peace in the last few
days.
He says he is exactly where he should be,
The place he's been travelling to get to his whole life.
My grandmother spoke those same words the day before
she passed.
Is it how you feel when you're not afraid of Death any
longer?

I scream "ceasefire now,' until I'm blue,
in the crowd of restless spirits.
They say our voices are just a flicker,
but when we stand together,
we turn it into a roaring fire.

When I return home, I watch "Born in Gaza" on Netflix.
At the end of it, a boy swims against soaring waves.
He dreams of life in the sea, life with no fences, fears or

worries.
They say every poem should end with hope –
I hope this boy still dreams.
Against all odds and soaring waves,
I hope his dreams come true.

Don't Cease the Human Heart

by INESSENCE

Dear God,

Our world is hurting, humanity aches,
Loved ones in pain too profound for tears.
Though we have all we need, their sorrow we partake in,
In a world where the end sometimes feels near.

God, the veils are lifting,
Great evil is in the open, no longer hidden.
Corruption roots deeper than we ever knew,
Governments with demonic entities, stirring feuds,
Fraying unity, sowing outrage and fear.
If hell exists, could it already be here?

Yet, beneath a cacophony of fire, screams, and tears,
Something profound is taking place.
It is the mass awakening of our human race.
A call to stand, mourn, and embrace our collective grace.
Today, we discover the power of our voices and faith,
In the quest for a world reborn from wraith.

But God, how will we heal from such deep scars?
The weight of massacre memories, too heavy to discard.
For now, we turn to you and pray,
Hoping all illusions yield to justice one day.

Hold tight, dear one, liberation is near,
In the darkest night, our innate light appears most clear.
Despite all madness, let's envision paradise possible,
After all, within us lies a power unstoppable.

The Country My Father Escaped After 30 Years Bombs Its Neighbour And My Mother Stays Quiet

by SVETLANA STERLIN

These days I'm in bed by 9 pm.
Rain lashes our thirsting yard
until the dead grass drowns
into its second death, and I'm asleep.

These days Мама doesn't get home
till 9 pm, when Папа turns on the TV
to blast a bomb raid siren
through the house. I wake

from the cusp of a dream and
for a moment, I'm afraid. I can't
move. Until Мама says, "Turn it down;
she's trying to sleep." The rain

lulls me back to a quiet state;
the TV's glow pokes through
my eyelids. I'm lying in my bed
in the tropical storm season's

humid half-light. All I have
is the knowledge that this weather
is temporary. And even if it's not,
Папа taught me how to swim

these waters. Not everyone
can say the same. Папа made sure

I knew why he left
and why he'll never return.

Bystander Effect

by SVETLANA STERLIN

It's four years later and I'm on a bus
while somewhere you drive your own car
and I stare out the window
at two women fighting on the street.
One has crutches. Both are pulling
each other's hair. They smack
down onto the concrete. I see a bag,
its contents spewed out all around
the bus stop. The driver does not
acknowledge the row. He dispatches
the lone passenger getting off,
a business suit who walks right past
the women. I turn my head and see
another passenger looking on,
mouth ajar, half-rising to their feet.
I let my face assume a frown
to demonstrate my concern.
One of the women looks at me then.
But the driver closes the door
and drives off.
And I know it's selfish and stupid of me
but the bus plows on and I'm not thinking
of those women, but of you.
Standing there, turning away,
walking on by, eyes down.
I turn to look out the window
but it's dark outside and I'm faced
with my own reflection. It's night
but the stars are hidden. The sky
is clear tonight, not reflecting anything.

Twilight

by BITHIKA HALDER

A deranged stillness
bedsheet dishevelled by afternoon nap
the fan gyrating at low on top—
yesterday, the sky here boomed of firecrackers,
elsewhere of death toll.

I open the windows
to birdsongs, closing them to twilight
calling birds back home, whilst
elsewhere, a land is waiting for twilight to befall,
to hear at the door, "I'm back home."

This City Does Not Deserve

by RACHAEL BUTTON

"This assault on its citizens, on its peace of mind,
on its sense of security,"
Governor Mills of Maine told flashing cameras.

No one deserves:
signs reading "Shelter in place"
sirens blocking streets
police guarding bodies,
uniforms shoulder to-shoulder
searchlights scanning cars.

A sign stands on Maine's border:
"Welcome Home."
Below it hangs, "the way life should be."
My uncle says every time he passes it on route
back to Bangor,
His shoulders drop
"Thank God we're home in Maine."

"No words can truly or fully measure the grief of Maine
people"
Mills said, voice steady, "This attack strikes at values we
hold dear for this precious place we call home."

For me, Maine is oysters,
sweaters, lichen-laced cliffs,
blueberry barrens.
For me, Maine is a cedar-shake cabin,
the first garden I planted
with my husband:
tomatoes mulched with seaweed,
arugula and purple potatoes edged with

with zinnias and calendula.

For me, Maine is Lewiston
where a sign canopies the Farmers Market
welcoming visitors in 18 languages.
Lewiston, where I would buy sambusas,
drink spiced tea, amble
brick walkways, tree-shaded sidewalks,
lined with textile mills.

Lewiston
where a white man
trained as a firearms instructor for the Army Reserves
killed 7 people at Just-In-Time bowling alley
and 8 at Schemengees Bar & Grille.

I imagine the jolt of gunshots.
          And...sirens?
                    Screaming...silence?

An assault on the peace of after-work beers
          balls striking pins,
          jukebox songs, sharing fries.

An assault on the peace of dropping shoulders,
          unclenching jaws,
          driving un-trafficked streets after summer people
leave.

All Thursday
community shelters.

          Waits
          for names
          of fallen,

longs to reshape lives that should be.

Ghazal: A Heartbeat for Palestine

by ZORA DE DREU

For three weeks straight now there have been people
marching for Palestine
There is always someone, somewhere, waving a flag for
Palestine

On the news I hear that one out of every three refugees is
Palestinian
And I imagine a web around the world of people from
Palestine

On every continent, in every country, in every deep dark
forest
There is now someone praying for Palestine

I wonder if the earth is vibrating from all that marching,
All the voices rising up from the streets, from Cuba to New
Zealand to Palestine

When I go to a demonstration, I see more children than I
have ever seen
At a protest, and I wonder what it does to their hearts to
march for Palestine

To shout Gaza Gaza, don't you cry, we will never let you die
To see their parents fight for liberation, to walk out for
Palestine

When we shout ceasefire now, I start crying,
I realise how literal it is, the fire being now in Palestine
The bombs are falling now, now, now
The heartbeat of the people is now, now, now in Palestine

And my heartbeat sounds like a prayer;

Please stop please please now we stand with you, dear
Palestine

Losing Ground

by SOFIA KALOTERAKIS

I had a dream that I was on the battlefield,
the ground shaking under my feet,
a momentary power display,
my weapon against yours,
my love against your hate.

For whom? For when? What do we fight for?

Leadership's charisma stops
when the earth prompts us to listen at noon,
and all sounds were once again soothed.

Assumption

by CONNY BORGELIOEN

Safe as houses must be
a misunderstanding.

Safe as houses lays claim
to a shrinking ground.

Safe as houses with walls as thick
as three holy books,

as houses that have not been stolen,
or claimed by someone else.

Safe as houses that still have windows,
that still have doors and roofs
and all walls standing.

Safe as houses that are filled with laughter,
with voices young and old,
with music and joy,

as houses not pockmarked
by another's disease.

Safe as houses is not to be
taken for granted.

It is not always granted.

We All Bleed The Same

by ESTHER MARIE

Bullets cascade like a waterfall.
Bombs burst, blazing their colours of fiery red,
Filling the sky like fireworks—
But this is nothing worth celebrating.
Disregard for human life.
The deceased line the streets.
Blood-soaked sheets where children once slept.
Bullet holes decorate the doorways of what was once a
home
Filled with joy and laughter.
These are the remnants of a war
That has never ceased.
If my arms could hold every child now motherless, they
would.
If my feet could walk into the fire and save at least one,
they would.
If my ears could hear the chilling screams of mothers
whose children are lost forever, my voice would never
stop screaming, and my heart would never stop praying
for peace.
We all bleed the same, but not all have lived through times
like this.

Futility

by JULENE TRIPP WEAVER

—After J.M.W. Turner, Strand bei Calais,
Fischerfrauen sammein Koder ein, 1830

Bent into our futile
tasks we miss the
sunset closing our
day. We sweat for
futile pennies weighted

with the width of the
world, its long wars
taking their toll.

A Call for the Lost

by JULENE TRIPP WEAVER

> for those taken from our families
> separated from our life
> by bullet or force.

Call in the angels to stand beside those
who run from the police with loaded guns

Call in the angels to soothe dying hearts
when we should know better than to maim and kill

Call on the angels to lie with the beaten and bruised
to run their healing ethereal hands over their open wounds

Call in the angels to embrace our loved ones
through their dying moments

Call in the angels to pray
Yes, even for the killers

Call in the angels who witnessed the lynching
who stood alongside those in the gas chambers

> —they understand the history carried in our cells
> they weep with prayer for each wounded heart
>
> they hold the hands of the children
> and the parents left behind
> offer nuggets of courage and faith—

Call in the angels because
our bodies are under attack
our spirit torn

children to men

by BETTA PELLEGRINI

look at the child:
wide, bloodshot eyes,
trembling lips,
muffled feeble cries.

if he dies?
he is only a child,
he is an innocent.

if he doesn't die?
how fortunate!
when his beard comes in,
the innocence leaves.

isn't it so?

or was the man once a child,
raised among bombings,
and death and destruction?

and raised too with beauty,
running, when he could,
among the olive trees?

but he dared to grow old,
and now he dares to resist,
to protect children of now
from bearing the same pain as him.

but he is a man —
can he feel pain?
is he not rough,

loveless?

after all, he is a man,
an Arab man,
a Palestinian man —
what is there to pray for?

he gives the shirt off his back
to wrap around a woman's head
as he leads her out of rubble;

he manages to hold gently
the child he carries
as he runs towards help;

he speaks sweetly
and praises God
over the noise of missiles.

he is the child you cry for,
grown up.

yes, he *was* a child,
but now he is a man.

he is twenty-four,
he can carry the weight
of this unjust world.

his voice is deep,
so he is to blame
for all he's never done.

his dark skin is wrinkled,
so he is unlovable:
no longer a pet,
but a horrible beast.

don't you know,
they're awful over there?
they'd kill you in an instant!
like we are doing to them.

close your eyes to their kindness;
see only what we show you,
carefully fabricated.

oh, they slither like snakes,
venomous!
they try to destroy
our destructive power!

run home, run home!
aren't you scared?
don't you see how violently
they beg to return?

run home, run home!
they are waving flags
and talking of freedom!

run home, run home!
they are holding keys
to the houses we stole!

run home, run home,
aren't you scared?
don't you see the child
has grown into a man?

blindfold

by BETTA PELLEGRINI

do you see them now?

will you keep your blindfold on
and your ears plugged
to avoid the sight of blood
and the sound of screams?

hands reach out
covered in familiar blood
but your manicured hands
are too precious to receive them.

i know you see them,
i know you hear them,
but do you have a heart?

will you care for yourself
so thoroughly
that you won't care for others?

and is it self-love
to forget humanity?

will you only use your voice
to recite a soulless eulogy
once it's much too late?

will you feign regret
and utter,
"we have failed you",
when you never tried?

or you could take your blindfold off,
or you could unplug your ears.

do you see the strength
amidst the horrors?

do you hear the love song
of resistance?

Afterwards

by DEVJANI BODEPUDI

Afterwards
sunbirds landed
refracting entire spectrums
thrown by water
as they bathed in
monument hollows
painting shadows with yellow and green
against fallen walls
freestanding doors.

City surfaces
shivered with pulsing and flits
as they sunned post-dawn
quilting the sky with their song
harmonising with deeper
modulations of the muezzin's adhān
from the one mosque that still stood.

From under the ruins
bodies rose that morning
to pray again
clawing their way into the light
blinking and stuttering
at the sight of sunbirds
and each other.

They embraced their fathers
and mothers and wives
and children and friends
and strangers
kissing plumps of faces
salt-dusty with relief
at being able to breathe

How long had they been asleep?

It wasn't important
because afterwards

like tens of thousands of sunbirds
startled to rise all at once
causing the ground to suck in its breath

war

like words
like hide
like loss
like resist
like fight
like mourn
like wait
like see
like watch
like chant
like grief
like song
like death

became sand held in hands
defying the shape of its container
spilling out from
vessels too small and cracked
with the weight

of a single rising.

Moon Over Palestine

by SARAH SANDS PHILLIPS

For some, the moon is an
opened eye

guiding us in the
darkest hours

For others, it pulls them to
their God

In a tidal locking
An infinite rotation

Dispelled and inconvenient
histories circle

Indivisible people
Indivisible lands

The lands below
unrest

pockmarked by bombs
in darkness

War-drenched and righteous
chants echo

from occupiers who are
somehow victims

Having learned nothing
from their own pain

The moon's face in full
trapped and hollowed

Our onlooking eyes
full of rage

black as night and
old blood

Truths rewritten
in darkness

by White merciless
gods of war

Under the watching

real violence

Cambridge, England

by JONATHAN CHAN

these knuckles were not chapped when
they clutched a rifle. it was the bite of a different
evening, breeze weaving
through patterned flesh. i fought the
crawling fear, the revolt in my stomach,
the prologue to days of echoing gunshots.
scarred targets could never shoot back.
my eyes never bled; my limbs hung
lamely on, never dangling from real
violence. game boys dreamed of
disassembled bodies.

a friend laughs as i flinch –
Arthur brought a gun to his temple.[2]

---

[2] *First published in going home (Landmark Books, 2022)*

in Myanmar they have come for the poets

by JONATHAN CHAN

and the students and the doctors and the
young. they have come to make targets of
toddlers and ash of teenaged girls. there is no
redemption in the razing of bullets, the tearing
of skulls, the puncturing of ambulance doors.
they have come for the nuns who kneel, arms
stretched from east to west, children cushioned
by shields of flesh, for the police who flee through
forests and rivers, horror laced in ribbons of water,
whispers echoing off mountainside crags. they have
come for the monks on procession, for cycles are
more than mere spasms. for how can a soul desire
nothing when there is nothing left to desire? they
have come to choke the throats that sing: their
noxious fumes that stun and blind, the mingling
of dust and the soot of books. in Myanmar they have
come for the poets: blood severed from the heart,
rivers cut open wide, unsent letters rattling in
emptied cells.[3]

---

[3] *First published in The jfa human rights journal.*

We Carry Our Dead

by SAPPHIRE ALLARD

The way we carry our secret memories,
Or our shy loves,
Or our souls,
Gently, lightly packed away in that part
Of us that nobody can take.
I've heard, though, that a certain type of wickedness can
take even this - that torture and war and
other unspeakable acts
can take even a person's soul,
after everything, after everything else
sometimes it is possible they take that too.
But
they cannot take the soul of the whole world,
not if we continue to speak
of the unspeakable things,
not if we in fact yell them in the streets,
even if we are not the yelling types.
Still - we must hold our cereal box signs
high above our heads,
play music with a beat,
know with certainty that this is protest
and dance is protest and
kneeling down right there on the street
is protest and love
is protest and defiance
and the word
NO.
No, we cannot make our
children come back,
all the children that were
always all of ours and
always a gift and

always a million times holier
and worth infinitely more
than any rogue deal that
could be conceived of by any
plain damaged angry men.
But we know this, don't we?
The most of us, ordinarily flawed and
ordinarily good people.
And we will continue to
sing this into the streets
and dance it in our kitchens,
whisper it in board rooms,
prayer rooms,
awkward family brunches,
until we can no longer
open our mouths or
move our bodies
that were never theirs to take,
not theirs to touch a single hair
or lay a single finger on,
but always ours, ours, to
caress gently, to embrace,
To love and to remember.

Disillusion

by YUKTI NARANG

Corpses grow
one upon the other in a mish-mash of names
and one name can mean many in a position like this
where open mouths are fed with dung in the name of food
grains,
and crops are bludgeoned before they reach the masses.

We preach and pray.
It does not appear in the papers or on electronic news
when barbed wires prick the mass of people.
Blood is not blood;
it is faux liquid,
spiced red.

When faces weep in the mornings,
tears are not tears;
they are warm water droplets from a faraway town,
away,
far away,
where we cannot reach.

We are not in trouble when we do not acknowledge them;
we are in trouble when we call them out,
for all the ember, the barricade,
is just a house lock –
nothing to be afraid of,
or is it?

Speak in Silence

by ELLIE DART

In time – blood will rot and words will scatter
to a hush. Peace means quiet, so they say.
Whilst bodies bleed time, we'll question
if it's read. When all the wounds are dressed
or buried, ghosts are left without tongues.
If stolen years become a minute's silence –
we'll never rest the dead.

Meanwhile the World Spins On

by NINA NAZIR

The holy land remembers the blood of its true keepers
as it folds them into its bosom.
Rubble of hearts and dreams
soaring heavenward, unrealised.
Children's dreams.
They write their names on the palms of their hands
so their kin will know they have left.

They search not for the best place to hide
but the best place to die.
Together, they huddle
in hospitals, mosques, churches.
These too will be crushed.
This, the experience of the other.

Fugitivity for the occupied
whose eyes search the graveyard
of the land they called home
suddened
unanchored
waiting to return
waiting forever.

Imams call out in the blackness of broken night
are met with cries of kin looking for kin
a dark night of souls
a clawing within.
The felled scape smells of casual death.
Flowers can't grow here.
Ghosts of ash in the breeze move on.
The ground is flesh-fertile and haunted.
The mourning sun lets nothing escape the eye.
Our collective consciousness.

Our collective conscience.

How lucky I am
not to be stone-hearted
to have a heart that shatters.
How lucky I am, my heart
is whole and beating.

Not in my name. Not in my name.
I am not silent.
I am not complicit.

Let us march.

You are mistaken, Mr Speaker.
You do not speak for me or them.
The masses have spoken without you
and they will take to the streets.

Again, again.

Until our siblings are free.

Free.

Free.

Meanwhile, the 'Great' in Britain
is a dark joke between capricious lords.

Meanwhile, the US tax dollar
continues to pay for death.

Space Invaders

by NINA NAZIR

The world is ablaze. Unrest unrests. Winter exits, slow,
blurry-eyed. Blossoms push through oblivious, say,
"What did I miss?" "Oh, nothing much," frowns Winter,
"just some madman wants a pan-Slavic universe
and sent a bunch of tanks to persuade everyone."
"Oh," says blossom, nodding, "What's a tank?"

"Hey," said the mercenaries, "Roll over."
"Be gone, demon!" said the people.
"You'll regret that," said the mercenaries.
"To the death!" yelled the people and charged.
Mercenaries climb back into their tanks, tutting
but momentarily thwarted.

Is change the same as transformation?
How? Why not?
The quandaries of skirmish.
The giantess of disorder.
The anatomy of the twisted days.

Russian soldiers swan into a house, frighten a woman's
elderly father. "Get out!" she screams, clumsily
brandishes a weapon she has never used. They look at
each other then back at her. "Relax," they say, "We're
only looking for food and smokes. Got any?" Hands
shaking, she gives them some and they leave. Fuming, she
glares lasers at their departing backs. The fucking
audacity.

Oh, but that was only the beginning.

Reliable Chaos

by SYDNEY CRUTCH

I've been angry.
Volcanic lava's found its way into my blood stream and is
boiling to the surface.
A steadfast throbbing, a reliable chaos sent to tip the
scales.
The injustices seem to pile up as the trees come down.
The people rise; words go unsaid and words are said with
knives.
The violence is so loud.
Another layer of the veil has been lifted from my eyes. I
was shielded from this world in more ways than I
contrived. Protected so I could collect some semblance of
safety to stand on as the waters rise.
And as they reach my eyes, the film is washed clean.
Revealing the same scene again but with brighter colours
and deeper pain.
A presence stands close by and asks me to protect life, to
speak for connection.
It requires such strength. To look the violence in its eyes
without letting it take me.
The presence asks me to love without discrimination, to
make choices outside the grip of fear, to remember the
power of this planet. I may be a voice for her, but she can
speak too. And she will not go gently.
I stand tall within the colours and assure myself I will not
leave their embrace again. I will find a way to fight for life,
feeling the pain when I must, but always from within the
light of love.
Letting go and letting Gaia work through me.
May the lava burn me clean from the inside out.
Ready once again to face the night.
Courage and strength to behold the day and dark without
veil.

Sipping each elixir as it lands before me. Medicine in every draft.
Respect for the dual, embodiment of unity, wisdom of the perfection that already exists, yet a knowing of my place on the scales.
Hand in hand.
I will not go gently.
We will not go gently.[4]

---

[4] *Lines inspired by Dylan Thomas' "Do not go gentle into that good night"*

Where Once the Flowers Grew

by CHAITALI SENGUPTA

When war's destructive hands tear the land,
like a hunter in rage, hope is then laid in a deep
dark cave. Hope... nailed in a coffin, collateral
damage, sighing under strange stars, lamenting
the stillborn dreams. Old and young in an aching
rollercoaster, drawn in the crosshairs of an appalling
march, only in one single file, through the bleak fields,
burning their identities. Deleted, littered, in the pile of
corpses!

The survivors, with their lingering scars, forever
chained, trapped to the demonic dance of memories,
exploding like dormant landmines. Each remembrance,
like a whizzing bullet, is a splattered tale of lost limbs.
A shrapnel called fear makes claw marks on their flesh.
Oh, winners! The heroes justifying wars! Did you not
know? No one wins a war! Unblinking, you stand like
Gods, rehearsing your high-pitched remarks on the
television screens, wrapping them in parchment, blowing
the bubbles of peace to the wind. The Fallible Gods! If
war is your idea to bring change, then who needs such
change?

Oh, victorious ones! Winner of wars, loser of
souls, no matter which treaties you sign,
with that heavy pen in your calloused hands,
all you leave behind is a land crowned with thorns,
smelling of gunpowder in the barren, blackened fields,
where once the gold-faced flowers grew.[5]

---

[5] *From The Crossings, poems on war, migration & Survival*

Whispers at the Well

by MARC SMEETS

'We need water,' her father speaks in a whisper.
The young girl puts on her cracked sandals and sighs.
Loneliness comes in many forms. Hers is a road, often
travelled. Motherless.
She sings a quiet song, painful memories abound.

The road that once was sand, is now dust.
The jar weighs heavy on her shoulders, as she walks to her
Golgotha. Her home is now the Place of the Skull.
Approaching the well, the Hooded Crow takes flight.

The water well surrounded, women wearing the black
hijab. Whispers filtering through the air.
Words of pain and sorrow.
The ancient olive tree bears its fruit, extends its branches.
The time for harvest is now.

Free the Land

by NJABULO NKAMBULE

All we need is a deep breath,
That sigh after we have had a long day.
Justice is not served anymore,
The law has its own friends nowadays,
Some people claim to be above the law,
Yet some get arrested for doing nothing.

Free the lands,
It is dressed in sorrow, tears and bloodshed,
Imagine waking up in the morning,
Only to fail making it to your bed in the evening,
But freezing in a mortuary,
With your flesh and bones freezing.

Free the lands
From this brutality, inhumanity we are drowning in,
Killing someone is just a chess game,
You don't get a sentence but to roam the streets free,
Protesting and fighting for your rights is a crime,
Fighting for democracy and freedom is a crime,
Are they enjoying seeing us cry?
This should be a major worry.

Free the lands from such cruelty,
Ignorance and arrogance are the most violent tools,
A leader can use to cause more riots in a state,
In times of unrest in a state,
There is really no room for throwing shades,
There is really no room for jokes and sarcasm.
If you are not paying attention,
Then really you don't want change,
If you are not angry with everything unfolding,
Then you've made friends with the enemy.

Free the lands from the hyenas,
From Napoleon and his fellow friends.
No government has ever won against its people,
Insulting the people you govern won't make you
triumphant,
Free the lands from the inhumane acts by security forces,
Don't they have relatives and friends?
What if this were to be done to their mothers, sons and
daughters?

This is the Armageddon of Africa,
A gravesite in the southern part,
People murdered like flies,
A person's life worth less than a penny,
These are not the lands our grandparents left us in,
These are not the lands our ancient kings fought for,
Greediness, selfishness and ignorance is the enemy of our
leaders,
Free these lands from such an inhumane doing.
Till we sing our last songs of revolution,
Blowing whistles, ululating and screaming,
Celebrating that we are free at last.

It Can't Be Unspeakable

by ERIN BROWNING

CEASE

amidst this unspeakable horror
each and every breath you have the privilege of receiving
implores you to find your voice.

CEASE

because the babies' weary lungs need a rest.

CEASE

because the mother's terror is unbearable,
as she sees her family pulled from the rubble.

CEASE

because the father's sorrow overwhelms you,
as dust sifts through his calloused fingers,
bloody from the futile salvage of his only known
homeland.

CEASE

because the anger in the son's eyes destroys you,
as he struggles with all his might to sort through the moral
conflict of
monsters we call leaders, sitting in their high rises,
speaking hate filled words into cameras
blasting into your screens,
their souls devoid of humanity.

CEASE

because the horror in the daughter's cries turns your
stomach,
as she recognizes her grandmother's long, soft hair
then scans to see her lifeless face.

CEASE

Scream your fury when you march in the streets,

SHUT THIS DOWN.

Speak your conviction when you have a conversation,

DESIST, DESIST, DESIST.

Whisper your love when you hold your Palestinian sister's
hand,

IT MUST STOP NOW.

Call It What It Is

by ELEANORE CHRISTINE

Noun, meaning the deliberate and systematic extermination
of a national, racial, political, or cultural group.

Call it what it is.

We think of this word as belonging to the past
accompanied by black & white photos
hollowed cheeks and sunken eyes
staring out of grim faces like living skeletons
a crush of humanity packed into train cars
iron gates, Arbeit macht frei, that are entered
but never left.

Call it what it is.

We said never again, never again
that history would not repeat itself.

Peace treaties were signed in the aftermath
but paper isn't enough to seep up poison
a poison that is hate, a poison that is intolerance
a poison that is extermination.

Call it what it is.

1945 wasn't the end, only a terrible beginning
Armenia, Bosnia and Herzegovina, Cambodia
Darfur, Rwanda, Myanmar
regimes have risen and are overthrown
democracies formed, fragile and factious
but always, inevitably, the cleansings continue.

Call it what it is.

I see images of Palestinians painted in blood & dust
hospitals and refugee camps bombarded each day
the white phosphorus gas
no food, no fuel, no medicine, no aid
nothing, nothing, nothing
a people abandoned and left to die
as the rest of the world covers its ears
blocking the sound of their screams.

What was the weeping mother's crime
the grief-stricken father's
the oceans of orphaned children
the entire lineages that have been erased?

Call it what it is.

Netanyahu cries that it is justice
Israel's government names it necessary
the military says it is self-protection —

no, no, call it butchery, call it catastrophe
call it massacre, call it nightmare
call it slaughter, call it a war crime.

And I think, even after all this time
we haven't learned a damn thing
about how to treat our fellow humans.

Call it what it is: genocide.

How a Refugee is Made

by ELEANORE CHRISTINE

What do you bring with you
when you're told to evacuate
when you don't know if you'll ever come back
If anything is still waiting for you?

You have only a four-hour window
a so-called humanitarian corridor
yet how can you be evicted from your homeland
when your roots stretch deep into the earth
down, down through generations?

It is not fleeing when there isn't a choice
it is forced removal.

If you don't leave now, you might never
so you must try to escape, you must
try to see another red-soaked, uncertain dawn.

Do you pack only the practical
whatever you can carry on your back
or clutched tightly in your arms
hopes and dreams left behind
for someone else to find among the ruins?

Do you take the family photo album
save memories no money can replace
do you let the birds and cats and dogs
try to fend for themselves?

How do you choose the impossible
which possessions to keep, which to abandon
like offerings made to the gods on broken altars
plucked from a life carefully and preciously built

a sacrifice of treasured things
to grant even the slightest chance
you might make it out alive.

You feel your tongue form the shape of a lie
tell your loved ones it will be alright
and perhaps you're trying to convince yourself, too.

How can you believe in peace
when your life becomes shrapnel
jagged and painful?

How can you believe in peace
when the world tastes like ash?

♮

Kites in Heaven

by ELEANORE CHRISTINE

On a day in late July 2011
12, 350 kites soared over Al-Waha beach
a new world record set by the children of Gaza
the most ever flown simultaneously
that hasn't been broken since.

I think about this moment, about what was achieved
Simultaneous. Unity. Together. One.
Something good. Something whole.

Perhaps the kite-fliers laughed
perhaps they smiled
perhaps they played, as youngsters do
perhaps they marvelled at all of the colours
at the rainbows dancing in the wind
perhaps they looked at the sky with joy and wonder
but that was then —

now the air is filled with bombs
now, kids write their names on their arms
in case their bodies are found, actively preparing
for their own demise
now, they dig themselves out of the rubble
are declared WCNSF
wounded child, no surviving family.

Now, over 5,000 of them have been killed
airstrikes turning children into corpses
and there will only be more tomorrow and tomorrow and
tomorrow, desperate pleas for a ceasefire
ignored.

Now, Gaza has become a mass grave

for the small, the defenceless, the innocent.

I wonder how many of the kite-fliers are gone.

I think of all the fathers, protective, proud, and strong
who can do nothing to stop the weapons of war.

I think of all the mothers, how they held their babies
in their arms when they took their first breath
how they carried them within their wombs
even before that

and how they cradle their little ones one last time
wrapped in white shrouds
singing a lullaby of tears
goodnight, goodnight
forevermore.

I hope there are kites in heaven
because they seem to have vanished
from this hell on earth.

House of Death: House of Cards in the Wind

by VAISHNAVI PUSAPATI

Once my eyes could see, there was nothing left to see.
Since they died in the bombing, they were already buried
when they were declared dead.
Death has a new postal address, he put roots down here,
to commute less to work, and it is called Gaza.
He is keeping his streak up here.
Do tears matter if there is no one to witness them?
Do people matter if they are just numbers in a tally?
After the bombings, when they died, they were already
buried.
In this town, the moribund people, with an appointment
with death,
Wait in short, staggering breaths, like jackfruits burst
open,
for he is too busy with others.
In this house of death, this strip, this ribbon of pain,
Old wounds haven't healed yet when new wounds open,
gape, puncturing people,
And a shadow has befallen, a shadow veil over the world
that
Refuses to see the tears, refuses to hear the wails,
Refuses to speak for the silenced, and the shadow
Is so big now, like a heavy, wet, blanket of blood, tears,
rubble,
The whole world plunges into tainted darkness.
"Are you pro-Israel? Are you pro-Palestine?" people ask,
Adding that asking for peace in the middle of the Middle
East
Makes no sense, saying it's not our war, adding, the rallies
Don't matter, halfway across world, my banner doesn't
matter,

And like Ukraine, like Armenia, like Syria, the globe shall keep
Its cadence, churning, and new news will displace old news.
Festivals will come and go. Celebrations, come and go.
But not me. I remain pinned on the wall, knowing death,
If we jump the map in skips of threes and fives, is our neighbour's neighbour.
His home right now, is an abusive one, burning, and I refuse to simply watch, voyeur.

Resolution

by N.T. ANH

May the spark in the sky we see
Fireworks
Of a new year, the birth of an era
Not dusted white
Burning us alive

We Don't Talk About War

by N.T. ANH

We don't talk about war.
It's a matter of the past.
It exists only in my mother's memories,
When she was 10, running from a bombed hospital.

We don't talk about the war.
As we've been through enough.
Mass murder, genocide, apartheid
Only exists in the history textbook.

But how strange to see them live on screen
Children burning, bodies in countless.
Cries, pain or joy divided by a wall,
By skin colour, by religion, by hatred.

We talk about the war.
It's a matter of life and death.
It exists in our time, ongoing, waiting to be ended.

Judgement in our reach, cease it with our hands!

So that one day, soon,
We don't talk about the war
But about how our days have been
How much hope we have
For the future, for freedom, for happiness.

I am Glad my Mother Did Not Live To See This Day

November 26, 2023

by RAYYA LIEBICH

I am reassured
my mother did not wake and read the headlines for 50
consecutive days.
She did not spend her days scrolling through images of
rubble, or holes through walls,
a mirror to the landscape of her own bombed homeland.

I am grateful
my mother does not have a heart in a body that could
break with grief
remembering her parent's summer home destroyed by
Israeli soldiers, her childhood years of war, every day as a
young adult holding the possibility of bombs.

I am relieved
free of a nervous system, my mother cannot feel a rage
that would electrify memories
after she fled as an Arab immigrant, where racism
followed her into a white privileged neighbourhood in
Montreal, and later in the neutrality of Switzerland.

I am comforted
my mother cannot weep at the sight of babies wrapped in
tin foil,
she is spared the umbilical trauma that these could
be her babies,
the way I imagine they could be mine.

I am thankful

my mother is liberated from this moment in history when
the bully was finally transparent enough for all eyes to see,
but the world hovered awkwardly as bystanders,
a reality where silence wins and those who speak are
punished.

May her spirit be free.
May her soul never witness what is happening with the
living.
May the cancer that stole her body be kinder than this
death she would have endured.

Dust

by KATE MARCHANT

She carried the weight of genocide
as she weaved reeds for her garden walls

Far away cries in her soul
as she yearned for the dirt on the soles of her feet to be clean

Yearning for a time when gazing through the leaves to the
sky was just that

When torture was not connected to her name

When walking the streets didn't have her in it staring back,
wrapped in blankets

And it would be lovely to write in sweet prose dipped in
honey. A feather in weight drinking lattes

But she can't forget the ones who suffer under the banner
she called home

Fellows that watch their cities crumble, their children
swallowed into dust

*

Tickets. She bought one and flew over layer upon layer of

cloud. Above the deep, rolling blue of salt

She arrived without borders, divvied out coloured pencils
to young children

Barefoot with big eyes asking for paper to draw their
dreams upon

With the sand on her skin she stood on sacred desert floors.
She heard the distance of war.

Held it close anyway and walked towards the mountains
with its wild sage and displaced poppies

Returning was what became foreign. Concrete and stone
and hard faces without questions

*

Gauze and tape by flashlight she bandaged the many
between tremors to make something in her lighter

As each explosion sucked up the air turning it to fear that
hung like wet cotton and carried like a current

While in hell she knew there was no other place she wanted.
Building back the discarded was the rebuilding of her soul

Doing something while running from deep nothing
A crevice in the earth that could swallow the world whole

And the Greek chorus called out their opinions at a distance as if there could be nuance in killing the innocent

*

When they said it was over she listened instead to the chirping of insects

A distraction from a proclaimed Armageddon void of reason. Her son implored why? So she told him

There would be no heaven when they had had so many chances with Eden

and now the rubble is a playground

Children make forts as they recall the family once buried there

Talking to ghosts as they make pretend cups of tea, the dust curls become steam

Their murmurings fill the pockets of grief with quiet musings and soft hymns

Carrying across a land stolen that never belonged to anyone but everyone... but especially them.

Those Wounded Wings in Nigeria

by MEREENA EAPPEN

Speaker 1:

Away, abode with heavy moroseness
and doubts in their hearts,
slain and slayed, not even their corpses
passed through the darkness of the Dark Continent.

Meshed walls, rocky floors, carved doors
and thatched houses invited them to the next world,
the world of pain, bars, and chains of civil wars.

"Liberate, Survive, Resolve,"
they speak from their hearts,
but there came none, oh! yes, there came
only a whip that was thrashed into their flesh.

Hurts and wounds, cracks and scars
earned the credits of power on them,
but they seldom gave up, fuelling their spark within.

Swollen faces, half-opened eyes
permute the softened air within the half-dead bodies,
reassured are their dreams, failed dreams,
and merely like a treasure in an unlatched casket.

The sun and the moon came,
one after the other, but not a man, woman, or child
were freed from the racial torture.

Speaker 2:

Can they reside in their soil,
can they engross that erstwhile life back?

Foresee the colonial power and anticipate
the leeway, let them not agonize any more.

The lull of night awaits the roaring echoes of gunshots
in the distance of painful death. Niger valleys
smell blood, and the morning mist turns red.

When you stir up or sojourn up nights on culmination,
isolate the thought that your loved ones are
here till very close to slavery/death.
Once you pucker your tackle and clutch the gun to fight
back, discern that you're a precious one for Nigeria.

Escape from there as you're crowded for home,
well! Deliberately look back and
know you weren't single-handedly.
When you appreciate collectivity and homeliness,
you may stay back from rivalry.

Images of boots and guns, breath and tears
float in the midst of the air.
Their hearts in void indeed uphold a silent prayer for
the nation fought and caught their spirits up high.

Speaker 3:

You contemplate reminiscences:
We can ponder about the forthcoming day.

When you guise yourself at war images and
see your companion back, better you smile
as your freedom is your existence.
Buzz your head up and evoke being full-bodied and
happy.
Open your eyes and see
the pain of the wounded and the dead.
"Please grasp on breath;
don't let rebels drive to your home."

Be coherent, sturdy, and promise that you can do this.
Your life will be filled with the frankincense of ecstasy.
I can recognize the burden you carry within.

You clasp your head great, but you scream inside.
I know your life as a warrior is not a laid-back one.
Recollections rendezvous a strong you!
You better stay stance and display no fear.
Overheard voices of your past in your brain cells.
You curiously have done effects inversely.
No other spell to meditate, you better respond peacefully,
the existence as a soldier is not a tranquil life.

The trauma of Nigeria is too ample to tolerate.
People are distressed, can't overlook the faces
that were lifeless nearby.
Oh! please remember! you are a fighter in life.

What Does It Matter?

by JP SEABRIGHT

What does it matter –

my petty pity poems
about pain and procrastination
perimenopause and porn and PTSD
I am alive and allowed to breathe
I can walk most streets without fear
I am not hunted for the colour of my skin
bombed because my God is different from yours
denied humanity for my gender identity
tortured for my political beliefs
ignored and taunted for being poor
locked away for being different
displaced into concentration camps for seeking refuge
discriminated against for being indigenous
a child taken from loving arms and homes
a woman jailed and forced to deliver her rapist's foetus
how can there be so much evil in a world so beautiful?
how can my words mean anything against
such an onslaught of hate and violence and destruction?

For this is the matter –

I can and will witness these atrocities
I must make myself watch
I will use my voice in peace and protest
and one day, the words will be written to condemn them.

What Happens

by ROBEL SANK

What happens,
when the live blogs stop.
When videos and quotes stop circulating
What happens,
when the algorithm decides
It's time for good vibes.

What happens to that pain,
hidden under the rubble,
Most of the time in plain sight,
that shouts for help.

What happens,
when newspapers lack
the ink for the truth.
When those who
you delegated
set the tone for
what is worth talking about.

What happens then my friend,
when you don't observe your surrounding
deeming yourself
immune to the suffering of others.

I quake for you and your
oblivion.
There may come a time
and I wish not
that your sufferings will also remain
a part of a broken screen
somewhere in the hands of someone.

Stop Killing People And Lying About It

by HOWARD YOUNG

Never mind that conversation
Dripping like blood onto the carpet
Soaking the room with propaganda
Or acting like a mask for the emitter
His sentences are the black fog of an
Un-costed response, silly words, nasty words
Sickly drop like syrup, from a wooden spoon
To glue the audience to a carpet of
Unacceptable conclusions.
Language has been poisoned
Like the rivers and the seas
Eroded of value like soils
And cut down low like
The forests and the woods,
All burnt books now,
A modern way of operating
Brutal, cold and calm.
Stories shiver on the bookshelves,
Poetry faces away,
Because their existence is threatened
By the burning of the truth,
A defiled host of terrible conversations
Dances in the open mouth of a perpetual lie,
Alternatives are being brought forward but,
Cracked bells have have a hollow ring
Broken mirrors always tell another story
Than the one you had thought
You had actually paid for.

Your Story Lives

by ALI ASHHAR

Generations will hear as
they carry forward the beacon;
the story will go on for
the name you left etched itself
on the chivalrous facet of mankind,
the kite in the sky beams
and gives a call to your son
as the scintillating sunray
of your persona touches its wing
your own flesh may not have seen it
but the pages of history will know;
generations will hear as
you left some unsold things behind—
where do they sell courage and integrity?

Fires Were Started

by JOHN O'HARE

Unrestrained flames lick languidly,
Consuming without appetite,
Dancing without rhythm,
But when there's a limited air supply,
An inferno builds momentum,

Millions are on the outside looking in,
Searching for meaning in a choked landscape,
Screams from the ground as new boundaries take shape,
Because even when deprived of oxygen,
There's a natural instinct to endure post-conflagration,

War is a crime dressed as politics,
It's a reminder of our weaknesses,
But narratives change through collective efforts,
And those frailties become our greatest teachers,
And at the very least,
An imbalance
Is somehow given permanence.

Bombed Away On Our Dime

by TIM MURPHY

So many
casually cheering
for a genocide,
so many others
floating in a sea
of their own silence,
apathy that drowns
another's humanity,
their right to live,
makes anything, everything
the war machine wants
socially acceptable,
even rewarded.

Like we learned
in school
just manifest
our destiny, the end.
The end, no matter the means.
Thousands of endings
written from beginnings,
no middle, no joyful last
moments of innocence
lost on their own terms,
no chance at a life
beyond their youth
bombed away on our dime.

Into Oblivion

by NYSSA MYEDA MIRZA

Yaaa Weldi, I sit here with all your *batanyat*, mittens, and
bonnets I made,
Filled with countless unfulfilled dreams for which I had so
heartily prayed;
Numb by your white, stained, airless *kafan* with no name
or tomb,
Remembering they said, no place is safer than a mother's
womb;
Yet nothing I did could keep you close to me or away
from harm,
Hearing the storm filling the void in my chest though I
may seem calm;
Mourning for the unsung lullabies, untold stories, and
games I couldn't play,
Being forced away from you and all that is you: this land
and the touch of this soft clay;

Away from all the tales of freedom and *istiqlal* I had been
told to believe,
Away from the memories, the nostalgia and the place to
grieve;
Away from Mama's makloubeh, Grandma's stories, the
neighbour's cat, Grandpa's olive trees,
Away from the orchard, having watermelon after school
with Baba in the warm gentle breeze;
Away from the lively alleys with dates' vendors, elderly
congregating over chai and children playing,
Away from the sound of church bells and azaan, now
drowned in blasts and the silent yet deafening praying;

The soundscape now engulfed with warning sirens forcing
us to go north,

And so the journey of despair and displacement continues
henceforth;
For it matters little to me whether we go north, south, east
or west,
It makes no difference as long as I can be near the place
you rest;

For I see neither the river nor the sea,
It is now a question of where I could be...

85 days into a genocide

by HANNAH LEVY

are bombs still falling?
my daughter asks
no mention of where
or who is doing
the dropping

do people survive?
my daughter asks
no mention of who
or what is doing
the living

but what about?
what about?
what about?
why?

yes, my darling
sometimes
I say

the answer
to why is
stuck
in my
chest

To be held

by HANNAH LEVY

The sky here glows golden dusk
and I wonder if it's sunrise in Gaza
when my child drops to hands and knees
over a monarch flattened on the street.
Its delicate hindwing is torn, severed
and she cradles this shattered symmetry
with two small palms in open prayer.
I graze its edge with the tip of my thumb
nearly detached from the delicate body
now no longer moving in her hands.
Can we save it? she asks, gazing down
and the back of my neck is cold panic,
water swells, lungs burn, tongue frozen.
I think *not me not this not now* but say

maybe we can try,
                    maybe,
        we can try.

I want everything that is broken
to be held with this kind of love.

How a Clock Works

by EDIE MEADE

Joy in wartime is breathing with a brick on the chest.
Laughter, kissing, happy new year

confetti for snow, chrysanthemum rainbows.
Suffocating horror. Broken children, I'm so sorry.

So sorry and so safe. Here,
the hands of a clock go on pointing

as if directing a kitchen or an orchestra,
as if already readying for the next celebrations.

Ten, nine, all together now. In our joy,
explosions come with a countdown

and our red seconds spring along
where your minutes lurch, where your hours creep.

They seem independent of one another
if you don't understand how a clock works.

Wondered How Birds

by EDIE MEADE

In the background, the way some people put the TV on to
go to sleep,
it got so I couldn't bear to be around a television,
tormented by its high electrical existence without volume,
across an apartment like that.

Across the world, there were people, peoples crying
over children, their children, and I couldn't stand
to either think about it or not think about it,
this baseline agony a navigation system of our species.

Thought about the genocide settling in
for the night, wondered how chimney birds who stopped
singing
held up when it turned cold, worried
about the stench of carcass wafting through the vents.

When we turned on the heat, it was maybe a mouse,
maybe
a bat or a bird, and we talked; we tried to figure out what
to do,
we did,
but finally resigned to wait it out.

How long could a small decomposition go on really?
I lit an angel-food-cake-scented candle that turned our
stomachs,
read local news about a young man gone
missing a month, how they found

he'd been trapped
all that time in an apartment building's chimney,
crying for help and neighbours called for help,

and when help arrived, it was cops.

Cops turned off
a television, screams mistaken for screams,
pleas for pleas,
it was some kind of mistake.

We haven't had a television in our house for years,
too much violence, too easy to off
one, I couldn't stand the screaming of a television
where real screaming was never shown.

Thought I could hear it even when the volume was down,
some people get so they can't sleep without it,
maybe they had birds in their chimneys
to drown out with the sound of human screams, maybe.

The birds went to sleep to the sound of us murmuring
sad news to each other in our bed,
I read the chimney article twice, why I don't know,
I guess I needed to get inside the horror again.

The man called for help again,
again the neighbours called for help,
then the cries went away,
but stench arose in their place, then leaks.

Horror returned its orders of magnitude,
the maintenance man sledgehammered the plaster,
and thought he found the tail of a dead opossum but
it was a shoestring glommed up with blood.

Listened for genocide on other people's TVs, wondered
how birds
could fly straight up a narrow flue, just
from nothing, flight,
wondered how that felt.

I lit the angel-food-cake candle, turned stomachs another night,
thought of the missing man and his mother,
she searched for him a month when the cops wouldn't,
put up missing posters she created all-caps,

with a picture of him smiling under mistletoe,
in flannel and Carhartt, her only child,
worried I was missing something,
wouldn't I want to know, or wouldn't I?

Read about the migratory patterns of birds,
their magnetic compass the Earth itself,
but how will we ever understand how,
did they recognise each other, how did they know?

Thousands of miles seemed so improbable,
but mostly they made it on the first try, right?
I wished humans had more instinct,
to protect them when nothing else did.

Found the missing man's mother's Facebook,
just post after post begging any tips, anything for him,
to come home or not come home if he didn't want to,
just let her know somehow he was alive.

She wouldn't bother him if he could just
give her a sign if he could just
give her some kind of sign, please,
please if he could just please.

Some closure she'd never bother him if he could just,
and all that time he was two blocks down,
down a chimney, trapped and nobody knew,
why or how he got down there.
It was some kind of mistake, his screams mistaken
for crime show reruns, and I couldn't stop thinking how,
mother and son were lost together,

all that time lost, cries going up at the same time, pleas for
pleas.

Please, please, just the way the birds peeped
in the chimney at night before they got quiet
about death, I worried for the loss of proportion,
blowing out the scale of mortality with war.

A stroke that takes out the language centre,
noticed, yes, but no, not right away, how the birds went
quiet in the chimney and wondered if they flew away
for the winter, some birds stayed but we didn't know
which kind

lived in chimneys, and we wondered if birds noticed
when one of the flock went missing,
did they keep count, did every bird count, the one who
broke a wing
and got left behind in the flue, did they realise

about genocide, I wanted to know even when I knew
knowing
would hurt me for suffering people, peoples pulled apart,
through peepholes I saw peoples being unpeopled,
mothers crying like their necks would break, children
limping, or limp.

In knotted sheets, it was like I couldn't turn it off,
it was an echolocation I couldn't unsense,
I read the news twice, once
on my phone and again in my head, a headspace,

crawlspace lit a cruel blue, and I could hear
the neighbour's television, the neighbour's
neighbour's true crime binge,
screaming the next building over.

A genocide is industrial,

death blowing out the scale at a stroke,
the word war warbles meaningless, and maybe
one difference between us and birds,

is where we have language, they have warning, or
is it where we have war, they have
to live with us.
Birdbrain death worry, me and who else could not flew
the flue.

I lit the candle, angel-
food-cake scent mingling with it, candlelight vigil for
ductwork,
unseen, given shape by stench, and read the obituary
for the chimney man, familiar with the pixelated gif of a
candle

on the funeral home memory book,
full of locals who went to school
with the dead man but they didn't really know
anything about him but his laugh, I guess.

He had an infectious laugh, and he loved to laugh
and joke, smile and laugh, and wasn't that something.
I took comfort in the tributes,
the way one single person could be missed,

mourned and honoured, how to mourn was to honour,
how each person filled a space,
and how good it was that people
who didn't even know the man could be sad,

could hold space for him
and for his mother,
who was sitting maybe in the dark somewhere,
a few blocks from me, maybe reading tributes, too,

in pixelated candlelight.

People could say even wrong things like,
"I have no words," or "goddamn, dude,
nobody should have to die like that."

RIP and a candle emoji, just
let me know if there's anything I can do,
or "there are no words, honey,
I'm so very sorry," just

sometimes there aren't words for the screaming
or the quiet after,
the quiet after,
the quiet after with an angel-food-cake-scented candle,

billowing in a draft, its wax sugar
icing a corpse, I read the tributes twice
and thought about genocide, and wondered how birds.

Motherland

SOPHIA MIHAILIDIS

our mother
embodied by the cedar tree
her roots spiralling
across oceans

the residue of her soil
flowing through our veins

she stands now
enervated by lamentation
the blood of her children
bordering her flag
as it quivers
against blackened sky

I Think They're Going To Bomb Beirut

SOPHIA MIHAILIDIS

We sit in the car, a long stretch of highway before us.
'I think they're going to bomb Beirut,' I say,
as if I'm saying that there might be traffic up ahead
or that the weather might turn later, should've brought a jacket.
'Yeah, I think so too,' he replies, a nonchalant response to a loaded gun
pointed directly at the foreheads of our ancestors.
And the way we speak about this, so casually, so effortlessly,
as if we are speaking about picking up dry cleaning or what we should eat for lunch
because we are so well-versed in second-hand devastation.
We are so used to calling our relatives
hoping that they are still alive to answer the phone.
We are so desensitized to the images
of our parents' hometowns, or what remains,
children trapped under collapsed ceilings, parents screaming for their babies,
piles of rubble and carcasses picked apart by the fingertips of the powerful.
And we watch as our people rebuild with hope, with faith, with purpose,
knowing full well that those dreams will be torn down
in a matter of time, yet they toil endlessly, rebuilding, reforming, resisting.
And we watch on, helplessly, as our motherland is decimated, year after year,
and we see your posts on social media, begging for sympathy for the ones
who are picking their teeth with the bones of our dead,

of our children, of our elders; of our future, of our history.
And we rage against the tyranny that is being flashed
across television screens
dressed up in a big bow, tears streaming down cheeks,
with a bomb clenched in their fist, hidden behind their
backs.
And we know, deep down, that had our parents not made
the sacrifice
to uproot their existences, to break their backs
to ensure a secure future for their children
away from the screaming citizens, the filth, the agony, the
inhumanity,
that we would be on the other side of the news coverage.
And we bless their diasporic heartache as they watch their
people die,
as they listen to the outcry in favour of their oppressors.
And we are so far removed from all of this,
living a privileged life, a blessed life, free from the shackles
of war.
We struggle to empathise with our own bone and blood
and our voices shake ever so slightly
when we are asked about where we come from
because we know that the answer will be met with lowered
eyes
and misguided assumptions about a peaceful people, a
loving people.
And we watch on as the country that our parents chose to
call home
lights their landmarks up in the colours of the flags
of those who reign terror upon us.
And our tongues are stuck, glued to the roofs of our
mouths,
because if we speak we will be called: racist, ignorant,
biased, uneducated,
and we are aware that we were born to march with the
losing side.
And we look at the sun, in the cloudless sky, wondering
why he never shines

upon the mountains and seas of our beloved motherland,
why he never shines upon the faces of those who need
him most,
why he never shows up for the ones who pray upon their
hands and knees,
no longer for peace, no longer for freedom, but for access
to the kingdom of heaven
because they know that is their only way to feel the
warmth of the sun again.
And we can't stretch our arms out across the oceans to
hold our brothers and sisters,
because we know if we did, they would cut them off too,
so we sit here, lingering in the awkwardness of our
privilege and our heartache.

A Pause is Not an End

by ELENA CHAMBERLAIN

A caesura, in a line of poetry,
is indicative. Telling the reader not
to rest, but to re-gather breath.

Oh! It may be: a break mid-metrical foot,
natural speech, a change of direction mid-walk:
heel toe heel toe heel. Toe heel toe heel.
The poet stops mid-line, and their words
change cadence. Their dance becomes stilted
in the shock of stillness, not long enough to let
another song take over. Instead,

the nib of a pen, or the press of a key,
folds that chosen breath into the fabric,
now writing faster to make up for each second lost.

Home

by HIBAH IQBAL

A hand-woven tapestry, gradually being unravelled thread
by thread until it is a mere pile of split threads.
A warm embrace of knafeh and a steaming cup of sage tea
ripple in fear with each sudden sound.
Open arms and the melodious call to prayer, five times a
day, getting quieter with each passing day.
Row after row of glorious olive trees on a sun-kissed
morning, plagued by snow showers of white phosphorus.
The buzz of 'merhaba' and 'Assalamu alaikum' amidst the
marketplace, replaced with trembling lips and the
exchanging of tears.
The beat of the tabla that once reverberated through the
heart of Palestinians, now silenced as their homeland
crumbles to ash before them.
Home is but a mirage floating within arm's reach,
overcome by the darkness of a senseless occupation.

100-Year-Old Testimony

by PALOMA GASKIN

I hear your name whispered
in hushed morning prayers:
A visceral connexion,
it's almost prophetic.

You cannot be blind
to the silent witnesses,
crowding on your path,
baring their unfreed souls,
with *gravitas* of presence,
hear them speak in echoes,
as they deliver, again,
100-year-old testimony.

I'm not old enough
to be unmoved,
or desensitised
in commemoration.

You are too young to know
what it is, to never forget,
a 'war to end all wars': WWI
how savage was the fighting,
on distant bloodied battlefields
of the Somme, Ypres, Dunkirk,
and in the forest of Verdun,
where tens of thousands
of bodies remain lost -
while their ghosts roam,
violently scarred landscapes,
forced to hold a toxic legacy,
as frontlines crisscross

with fault lines of power,
in stasis for a higher purpose:
To elicit your remembrance,
for even two minutes.

We fail to contemplate the cost,
if our sole education comes from
cinematographic reconstructions,
conjured up to excavate
rifles, rosaries and tobacco tins,
like keepsakes of horrors -
fallout from enduring conflict
persists, if we keep denying
the institutional prejudices,
stalking our possible futures.

It would serve us now,
to become more mindful
of our collective history,
instead of being distracted
by global-stage political histrionics,
raising up the ugly head
of nationalism in Europe,
vast tracts of emotional poison
opened up to heal, once and for all,
no longer festering concealed,
in our uneasy, spoilt lifetimes,
leading us to the edge,
kicking and screaming
as default resistance fighters,
to the brink of the hate precipice.

We live in a shell shock culture,
that values fake perception
over authenticity and truth,
as if kindness were a weakness,
and vulnerability is a shame,
though still, I believe in humanity!

Must we keep choosing conflict?
Surely we understand at last,
every war is the unwinnable kind:
It's dangerous to think otherwise.

I want you to live, please,
break the stuck record,
of your repeating mistakes,
for which I'll pay the price.[6]

---

[6] *First published on hitRECord, 2018.*

Children

by AJ WOJTALIK

my brother did the math
as fast as he could but
the numbers outrun his pen
still
death toll scaled
so we can see blood
saturated soil
in terms of our own faces
lest privilege become permission
to ignore
the sacred universal constant
keep our children safe
keep all children safe
that they may become the elders
who do the same

Pause

by KAREN FRASER

And yet, there was no relief. Only anxiety
knowing it would begin again with a vengeance-
the endless stream of brutalising ceaseless fury,
witnessing the devastation, the trauma
escalating every day without abate.
Eyes filled with death. Psyches bleeding out.

And yet, no pause in othering,
in self-righteousness and propaganda,
in the determination to clear the view to the sea,
in the endless bin-fire of colonisation.
Every opportunity taken to set scenes of vindication:
a blackboard, a hospital room, every child- Hamas!

And still, powerless to make it cease. Alone-
posting, calling, emailing, reasoning, marching
begging for a shred of human decency, for freedom,
to spare each precious life, every sweet baby.
The rage of desperation made 'unalive' in deaf ears.
History looping daily on repeat, maddening the heart
as victim becomes perpetrator with a free pass.

And yet, we do not die. Yes, we tire
in a persistent desire for dignity and respect to triumph.
We answer the call to rally beside the powerless,
to lay comfort, discomfort and privilege on the line,
to speak truth to power and walk in solidarity
against the maniacal might of money and greed,
determined that all should live fully, safely and
in the highest regard, even love, for one another.

My Words in Fragments

by DIANA WIESE

My words in fragments
like scattered pieces of
former homes
hospital rooms
families

My words about
a bird snatched
from its nest,
babies torn
from their beds

Words about
a tunnel system
underneath their cribs
for men in power sitting
on their asses in a safe place
claiming their people
take pride in being
human shields

They do not get to choose

My words about
the unprotected and the armed
About
guilt struck pledges

About
hungry little bodies
who will remember it as
the disease of fear and revenge

creeps into every cell

About
babies' broken bodies
humans' broken hearts

About
losses, losses, losses
of lives and opportunities for peace

About
wanting to be cycle breakers
wanting this terror and genocide
to STOP

In the Pits of Misery, I Drowned

by ANOUSHA RAFIQ

I stared at her eyes
For as long as I could.
Her lashes soaked in tears;
Like the hands of tyrants, bathed in blood.
She kissed her brother's hand, one last time
Just as she kissed her mother, one last time.
Just as she kissed her sister, one last time.
How do you cope with the void one feels when a beloved
leaves?
How can a heart beat,
knowing that the very womb that birthed this bosom had
cruelly been killed?
She will fight till the end,
Her tears will get dry,
Her voice will go silent,
The world will label her resilient.
Oh, conscienceless world!
What option do they have?
Instead of being a rock,
For you have left them alone,
To die one by one.
What choice do they have?
Other than to wait for their turn.
No umbrella will save the world from the livid rain in her
eyes. It's just a matter of time,
Oh, forgetful world!

Are These Words From Gaza Reaching The World?

by ANOUSHA RAFIQ

"He wasn't a part of me; he was all of me."
"How many times should I die before I die?"
"In one day, they killed every member of my family.
In one day, everyone I loved was wiped out.
I am left all alone."
"Is this message from this kid in Gaza reaching the
World?"
"When will this end?"
"I can't keep filming this.
I can't."
"The whole world suddenly died; I knew my brothers
were under the rubble."
"I became a body without a soul."
"Why are you silent?"
"To whom should I embrace?"
"I feel like it would be better if I had died with my mum."
"I do not want anyone to ask me about my childhood
anymore. I have no childhood."
"I do not want anyone to ask me about my mental health.
It is gone."
"If we are for ourselves alone, who are we?"
"Do not call us legends; we are human beings."
"We will not flee."
"We will not retreat."
"Why are you silent?"
"Don't we deserve some humanity from you? To establish
a ceasefire?"

Recipe for the Winter Solstice

by ELOISE ARMARY

Unroll the puff pastry,
a Palestinian mother's cry seasoning the base.
Pour the olive oil onto the pan,
while she keeps the last jar of olives
as a reminder that her culture is real.
Slice the bacon in dice,
thankful for the pig that was sacrificed
for your plate.
Tune in to her louder scream,
in despair for being valued less than an animal.
Cut the leek and garlic,
throw into the mix. I don't know
what she is digging to feed her children.
Spread the garnish onto the cut pastry,
add cubes of cheddar and fold the bakes
onto themselves,
close your eyes and picture
her family tight in between her arms.
Slide the tray into the preheated oven
at 200 degrees Celsius,
they are looking at the sky for any warnings
of bombs tonight.
Think of the Earth at its farthest distance from the sun,
thank everything and everyone involved
in the making of this meal, and start the search
for our lost shared humanity.

Projectile Rage

by HELENA LYON-SHAW

Lately, I have been dreaming of rebirth,
of the way I wanted it to be
Containing my wishes and hopes
of a tender and present moment of joy

Now I think of you sisters,
with the same hopes and dreams
From that first butterfly flutter,
to here, with abandoned hope

Any sense of safety, gone, with a sky that is on fire
A woman's womb housed you all
Her pain gave life to you
And now you destroy her dreams?

The rage in my ribcage,
the imagined pain,
is not suitable for print.

What can I do for you, sisters?
With silent tears and orange hues,
Wishing you dreams of rebirth
No one can take that away from you

Lament for Gaza

by REBECCA RIJSDIJK

If the Germans had won the war,
The Allied forces would be labelled terrorists.
The atomic bombs dropped on the Japanese would be
recounted as the worst terrorist attack in human history.

The victor shapes the narrative.
One person's terrorist is another person's freedom fighter.
Violence begets violence, but for non-violence to work,
your opponent must possess a conscience.

The Oppressor's propaganda machine wants you to
believe all Muslims are Hamas and only Jesus will save us.

Plot twist: Jesus was a brown-skinned, undocumented
Middle Eastern migrant.

The millionaires play their tunes on Fox News:
Netanyahu, with a net worth of 80 million dollars, claims:
"We did not start this war, but we will finish it." He
neglects the 75 years of illegally occupying Arab land.

Joe Biden, worth 10 million dollars, seems ready for a
nursing home as he voices support for the Israeli
government. Sniping kids in Gaza is self-defence, after all.
Good dog, Joe. He secures some natural gas reserves in
return.

Labour leader Starmer, worth at least 7 million pounds,
views cutting off power and water to the entire Palestinian
community as justified. Can't blame the bastard – it works
wonders for him back home. Piles of worn-out blankets,
ice flowers on the windows, food stamps, and mould. But

at least the foreigners are gone. Keep calm and condone a
fucking genocide. God save the fucking King.

For those who stayed silent, let me explain once more:

Bombing hospitals is bad.
Killing babies and old people is bad.
Shooting white phosphorus at civilians is bad.
Genocide. Very fucking bad.

"That headscarf-wearing animal is trying to take your
cookie," the billionaire whispers to the labourer.

I watch Gaza's skyline reduced to ashes until I finally pass
out.

Hunger

by MATTEA GERNENTZ

We are falling awake, whispering
get well soon and exiting Zoom.
I have been to as many weddings
as funerals, but they both have a wild
annihilating light. I know I'm not done
living yet, but I'm no longer a child
and how am I supposed to live without
wonder, popsicle stains, striped kneesocks?
I used to gaze at the moon from the backseat,
like a distant pale balloon tethered to me.
How can we live without being sought,
without ever being found? Underneath a post,
harsh words without presence: *kill yourself.*
Men in my DMs daily, formulating excuses
to love me, crooning sycophants, mad.
Oceans rising, too late and too soon,
plant-based menus as clairvoyant runes.
I remember catching fireflies, the grass
above my knees, but now that home is sold.
The bugs are dead, dying. Tenfold, they said
the world would end, but we're still here:

                              this famine is our daily bread.

Not Even the Cats

by ALLY EDEN

have enough clean water to survive.
A falling sky can make a whole family

disappear. So many people I love
swept and hollowed
into the archives. History

a prisoner of spoiled money.
Tell me it's not another shrouded
infant but cocooning butterfly.

Tell me the streets are lined with
butterflies & they will fly, they
will rise. We wake

to see who is still alive.
We watch the news & tainted
news. Every bomb burst

blooms endless
onslaught of colonial genocide.
Medics mothers & prayers

all harvested in the wild
flower nations. The long shadow of
democracy looms

horrified. All my friends pump the bellows
& half the shape of fire
burns on the other line.

Tell me what do we do now
with all these children.

Death still hanging like a locket

greens my clavicle,
the outer edges of language,
green the grapes swelling on the vine.

Somewhere a pomegranate,
somewhere a kitten,
somewhere a bleeding eye.

Tell me this is how it starts—
free Palestine,
free Palestine.

A Poem in Praise of Life

by MEHRNOOSH MAJARI KASMAEI

A broken body,
half burnt,
under the debris.
It was Ahmed, the jolly boy,
Ahmed, there he is, our neighbour's son,
the restless boy,
playing in the alley the day before,
kicking his colourful ball.

I cover my ears with my hands,
feeble and shaking,
the hands once full of life,
for not going deaf by the uproar of rockets sent to our
site.

I cover my ears with my hands,
for my drumming pulse not to rip apart the thin texture of
silence,
a short solitude before nothingness,
before my departure.

I'm destitute for a moment of quietude.

In my very last poem, I versed,
calling my brother on the other side of the wall,
beyond the unseeable horizon,
where the earth is still fresh,
and the sky bereft of the sharp, sparkling red of mortars,
still clear blue,
and the soil has not yet gone mad, thirsty with blood,
where poems are lacking the smell of festering scars,
and on the tapestry of life,
there are still colours shining.

A world where Ahmeds do not remain under the rubble,
they run, in the generously expanded fields and meadows,
singing endless cheerful songs
about freedom.

I told my brother my time has come,
very soon.

Perhaps I will join the young Ahmed,
running along the fields of liveliness,
donned with the greenery of life,
unstained by the fresh redness of blood,
and I sing my songs
because we are not born to suffer,
we are born to live.

Because this is what we should sing
and verse our poems about,
about the colours of life.

I'm eluding the alley, and its horrifying sounds.
It squeezes my inflamed heart
so that my chest burns
like Ahmed's burnt body,
left under the debris.

Soon, it will be over,
and with a press of a finger,
my brother from beyond the border
will spread my distressed words to those lands
where no one's ever been afraid of decaying burnt bodies,
never...
to those warm, bright homes void of the bangs of
machine guns,
non-stop shooting,
at the endless enmities of generations upon generations.
From the deep-rooted loathing of the hearts,
into the swelling hatred of forgotten years to come.

From the half-opened windows gliding on their rusted
hinges,
full of cracks,
shattered,
for years and years and years,
the only deafening music of our land,
all behind the tall cemented walls,
so long
that even the sun is not allowed to cross.

A land without sunrise
and sunset,
without light.

They are shooting from both sides of the street,
and iron bullets
with speedy beats
are targeting Ahmeds
in the middle of the fields.

They are shooting from both sides of the street,
and I...
have forgotten where the enemy stands,
on which side,
because they are shooting from both sides,
and there are bodies in the middle of the field,
on the grey trail, where Ahmed used to play once,
gleefully kicking the ball.

The bodies lie in the middle,
like leftover lumbers eaten by termites,
pushed into oblivion,
and no one knows where the enemy stands,
on which side of the road.
And all the exits are barred,
entrances obscured.

Where does the enemy stand?

On which side?

It doesn't matter anymore.
It never mattered to Ahmed
because there are bodies in the middle of the road,
like the abundance of termite-eaten lumbers,
forgotten.

They are shooting from both sides of the street,
and iron bullets
with speedy beats
are targeting Ahmeds
in the middle of the fields,
and I...
have forgotten where the enemy stands,
on which side.

No friend has been left anymore.
I stopped looking for them long ago,
and the wailing of Ahmed's mother
is the only sound of the alley left behind,
torn into a thousand echoing cries.

I have covered my ears with my hands
because no one will call my name anymore.

Cries will remain amid the blocked-out alleys,
but an echo will abide,
and it reflects from the cemented tall walls and fences so
long
that perhaps one day,
a day when the fake friends and enemies had left us alone,
the wall will break apart.
Yes, I hear the pulled trigger from the alley,
shoot...
and a rocket on its way.

Like a shooting star blazed with doom and demise.

I know,
this time, I know,
with the morbid optimism of a convict to death,
that this time, my ceiling will collapse,
and my burnt body will remain under the rubble.
Listen... it's coming, the whistling of my demise,
but I versed my last poem
in praise of running freely, playfully,
chanting cheerful songs
beyond the cemented tall walls,
along the rolling green hills,
and expanded endless meadows of vibrant lands,
where the earth is unstained
and the soil is not thirsty for blood.

A poem in praise of Ahmed's careless laughter,
still echoing among the debris.
A poem in praise of life
from an impossible time
when alleyways were still a place to be alive.

Acknowledgements

As the founder of Sunday Mornings at the River, it is both an honour and a privilege to present "Songs of Revolution," a compelling anthology that speaks to the resilience of the human spirit amidst the tides of history. This collection would not have been possible without the passion, talent, and dedication of a remarkable group of poets who lent their voices to this cause.

I extend my heartfelt gratitude to each poet, listed below, for their invaluable contributions:

Ahmad Morid, AJ Wojtalik, Ali Ashhar, Ally Eden, Alshaad Kara, Anne Fey, Anousha Rafiq, Ava Mahtab, Betta Pellegrini, Bithika Halder, Chaitali Sengupta, Cindy J. Steward, Conny Borgelioen, Devjani Bodepudi, Diana Wiese, Edie Meade, Eleanore Christine, Elena Chamberlain, Ellie Dart, Eloise Armary, Erin Browning, Esther Marie, Fi Dignan, Fidan Nazim, Giacomo Boffi, Hannah Levy, Helena Lyon-Shaw, Hibah Iqbal, Howard Young, Inessence, Jodie Duffy, John O'Hare, Jonathan Chan, Joseph Nutman, JP Seabright, Jude Raed, Julene Tripp Weaver, Julian Bond, Karen E Fraser, Kate Marchant, Marc Smeets, Marcella Cavallo, Mattea Gernentz, Maureen Tañada, Mehrnoosh Majari Kasmaei, Mereena Eappen, N.T. Anh, Nina Nazir, Njabulo Nkambule, Nyssa Myeda Mirza, Paloma Gaskin, Rachael Button, Rahul Singh, Rayya Liebich, Rebecca M Winter, Rebecca Rijsdijk, Robel Sank, Roy Duffield, Ryan Schulte, Sapphire Allard, Sarah Sands Phillips, Sofia Kaloterakis, Sonia Hadj Said, Sophia Mihailidis, Svetlana Sterlin, Sydney Crutch, Tetyana Denford,

Tim Murphy, Tonkabell, Vaishnavi Pusapati, Yukti Narang, and Zora de Dreu.

Each one of you has played an integral role in bringing this anthology to life, and your words are not just an expression of art but also a beacon of hope and solidarity.

I would also like to highlight the commitment of Sunday Mornings at the River in supporting humanitarian causes. We are proud to announce that 100% of the royalties from "Songs of Revolution" will be donated to Medical Aid for Palestinians, an organisation dedicated to providing health and medical care to those affected in the region. This decision underscores our belief in the power of literature not only to inspire change but also to make a tangible difference in the lives of those in need.

To our readers, your support extends far beyond the pages of this book. By embracing "Songs of Revolution," you are contributing to a cause that transcends borders and unites us in our common humanity.

Thank you for being part of this journey.

About the Publisher

Sunday Mornings at the River is a poetry publisher that is dedicated to elevating and amplifying the voices of poets who are often marginalized or overlooked by the traditional publishing world.

At Sunday Mornings at the River, we are committed to creating a thriving literary community that is based on healthy and inclusive collaborations. We believe that everyone has the right to be heard, and we strive to provide a platform for poets to share their work with a wider audience.

Our focus is on publishing poetry that is thought-provoking, challenging, and that speaks to the unnameable aspects of the human experience. We believe that poets have the power to name the frauds, take sides, start arguments, and shape the world, and we are always on the lookout for new voices that are pushing the boundaries of traditional poetry.

As an independent publisher, we are dedicated to promoting equality and inclusivity in all our endeavours. Whether we are working with established authors or helping emerging poets to get their work out into the world, we committed to creating a welcoming and supportive environment for poets of all backgrounds and experiences.

Index

Scan me
for more books
by Sunday Mornings
at the River

w: sundaymorningsattheriver.com
e: hello@sundaymorningsattheriver.com
ig: @sundaymorningsattheriver

Printed in Great Britain
by Amazon